Jack McKeon:

Baseball, Cigars & Saint Theresa

A Collection Of Rare Photos, Trivia,
Interviews, Quotes And Much More........

To Tom.,
Best Wishes to
a great guy!
Tom Beukard

Jack McKeon

Jack McKeon:

Baseball, Cigars &

Saint Theresa

A Collection of Rare Photos, Trivia, Interviews, Quotes And Much More........

By Tom Burkard

Mr. Opportunity Publishing

A Mr. Opportunity Book
Published by Mr. Opportunity Publishing

Editorial, sales and distribution, and rights and permissions inquiries should be addressed to Mr. Opportunity Publishing, PO Box 3027, South Amboy, N.J. 08879

Cover Design, and Photo Scans by Brian Stratton, Scans & More

Manufactured in the United States of America

Burkard, Tom
    Jack McKeon: Baseball, Cigars & Saint Theresa/ By Tom Burkard
    "A Mr. Opportunity Book
    McKeon, John "Jack," 1930-Baseball manager, general manager, etc.

2004

Dedication

This book is dedicated to two of my dearest friends in the world, former major league baseball player, Allie Clark, and Dr. Kenneth Benson, a retired Department Chairman of Health, Physical Education & Recreation at Kean University in Union, New Jersey.

Clark holds the distinction of being one of only two major leaguers in history to have played on two different World Series Championship teams in his first two years in the major leagues. He was a member of the 1947 New York Yankees, and 1948 Cleveland Indians, who won it all. Allie has always been gracious and helpful with any baseball projects I have pursued over the years, and is a true credit to our community of South Amboy, New Jersey. He remains active in all local events, including youth league baseball, and at 81 years young is one of the most-respected and popular men in our hometown.

Dr. Benson has been in the educational field his entire life. Immediately after serving in World War II, he began teaching at New York University, where he remained for many years. He then took a teaching position at Newark State College, which later became Kean University. At Kean, he served as the Department Chairman of the Health, Physical Education and Recreation Department, in charge of 40 professors and educators. He is also a highly-recognized author of five books dealing with recreation and crafts for the handicapped.

Ken has been an advisor, consultant, inspiration and more importantly, a wonderful friend to me through all of my journalistic endeavors.

A young 86, Dr. Kenneth Benson keeps very busy and loves to travel, especially to New Hampshire to visit his son, Governor Craig Benson and his family.

Allie and Ken, thank you both from the bottom of my heart for believing in me and always being supportive and helpful. You are two of the greatest people I've ever known in my life. May God Bless you both, always!

Contents

1935-Four year old Jack (l) and his brother Bill (r) all dressed up.
(Photo courtesy of Bill McKeon)

Introduction

As a youngster, Jack McKeon always had a dream of playing professional baseball. He achieved that by catching in the minor leagues for many years, and then after realizing that he would not make the majors as a player, shifted his dream to becoming a big league manager. He reached that goal as well, and again, refocused his dream, this time to managing in the World Series.

Jack McKeon is a firm believer that dreams really do come true. He also sincerely believes in the power of prayer. In 2003, after more than 50 years in professional baseball, he took over the Florida Marlins on Mother's Day, instilled a positive attitude and improved the team's work ethic, while turning them into bona-fide winners and eventually World Series Champions. An outstanding inspirational and motivational speaker, McKeon tells listeners his story, that "Everyone has a dream. Dreams really do come true. Through hard work and dedication anyone can make their dreams come true." Jack's dream once again, really did come true.

McKeon is also known around the baseball world as a person who really enjoys smoking cigars, almost anytime and anywhere. One of my all-time favorite quotes from Jack to me after I asked him if the cigars I had given him the previous day were any good, was, "There's no such thing as a bad cigar."

Jack is also a religious man, and attends daily Mass, no matter where the team is playing or what town he happens to be in. His favorite saint is Saint Theresa "A prodigy of miracles," whom he prays to all the time, and credits with his return to baseball, and winning the World Series in 2003.

How did Saint Theresa come into his life? "When I was managing at Cincinnati, I went to church one day, and a fan had seen me at church on a daily basis, and he came up to me and said, 'I got a pamphlet I want to present to you. It's my favorite saint, and she's the prodigy of miracles in the Catholic Church.' I took that little card, and from that day on, I've been working on Saint Theresa. I've gotta believe that if it wasn't for her, last year, we would never have made it to be World Champions," said McKeon.

Jack's managerial genius and strategic moves carried the "Miracle Marlins" over the heavily-favored Barry Bonds led San Francisco Giants, and also past the pitching plentiful Chicago Cubs team that featured home run threat, Sammy Sosa in the NLCS.

The rest is history of course, as Florida captured its elusive dream by defeating the almighty and usually invincible New York Yankees, four games to two. McKeon's decision to pitch ace Josh Beckett on two days rest was a gutsy move to say the least, but turned out to be one of the most brilliant gambles in all of Major League Baseball in 2003. Baseball experts and critics openly ripped and scorned the manager's move, but were quickly silenced, as Beckett was outstanding, and defeated the Yankees to clinch the title.

It was a long and winding road to the World Series for Jack McKeon, in which there were many stops along the way. Jack bounced around as a catcher for 10 years and later a manager for nearly 20 years in the minor leagues before getting his big break in the major leagues with the Kansas City Royals in 1973. He also had managerial stints with the legendary Charlie Finley's Oakland A's, the San Diego Padres and Cincinnati Reds, where he guided Cincy to 96 victories and a second place finish in 1999, while garnering the National League "Manager of The Year" Award. The following year, the Reds came in second place again, and McKeon was fired.

Jack went back to his North Carolina home, and for over two years felt that his baseball career was over. After all, who would take a chance on hiring someone over 70 years old? Well, his prayers were answered, and the Marlins called him to revive their floundering fish at Miami. The rest is history, as he became the oldest manager in baseball to guide a team to the World Series Championship. In the off-season, he racked up countless awards and honors, with the most prestigious being the 2003 National League "Manager of The Year" Award.

Writing *Jack McKeon: Baseball, Cigars and Saint Theresa* has been a labor of love for me. Jack is one of my closest friends in the world, and I consider him family. He is by far the most interesting person I have ever met or interviewed. Since 1999, I have visited him many times at ballparks throughout the country, for interviews and photo shoots, and have always found him to be helpful, insightful and accessible, "the media's dream."

Jack certainly has a big heart, and despite his worldwide fame is always ready to help someone or organization in need. A native of my hometown, he has been living in North Carolina for over 50 years, but in early 2000, came back to help our First Aid Squad at a fundraiser, by being the featured guest signer at a sports card/memorabilia show, and later at a sports auction. McKeon is a first-rate, class act all the way!

So what else is there about this 73-year old veteran of many baseball wars that makes him so special? Jack McKeon is the greatest people person I have ever known. He knows how to read people, and more importantly how to treat them. One of his greatest gifts is that he can make someone feel like they are the most important person in the world. Outstanding charisma! Jack certainly knows how to motivate people and get the very best out of them. I'm talking about the average guy or girl on the street, to fans, players, even corporate executives, and everyone in between. Jack takes a genuine interest in you, and really makes you feel good about yourself.

I will never forget how important he made me feel when I called him after the World Series to congratulate him. Jack said to me, "My only regret was that you weren't here with us so you could hoist the World Series Trophy and join in the celebration." That's Jack, always concerned and caring about the other guy.

McKeon is truly a master psychologist, as well as an inspiration, now more than ever, especially to senior citizens throughout the world. His zest for life, and determination to enjoy it and be successful, are a true treasure to behold. The energy level that this man displays day in, and day out is incredible and unsurpassed by most 70-year olds, and even people half his age. His sister Marge says, "He's like the Energizer Bunny." Jack is dedicated to his family first, then the team, and baseball, where he is one of the greatest ambassadors in the game today.

A fiery competitor, who knows the game inside and out, he's the kind of guy you want in your corner when everything seems to be going wrong. Jack always seems to be cool, calm and collected, and have the situation under control.

I remember meeting Jeffrey Loria, owner of the Marlins for the first time in the dugout at Shea Stadium in August 2003, a month or so before the club battled for the Wild Card playoff spot. I congratulated him on the team and the fine job that Jack was doing, and he said, "My only regret is that we didn't get Jack sooner."

McKeon's not afraid to gamble or take a risk, such as when he pitched Beckett in Game 6 of the 2003 World Series, or moving Miguel Cabrera to right field to replace a slumping Juan Encarnacion late in 2003. Also consider the faith he had in young Cabrera by batting him in the cleanup slot throughout the playoffs and World Series against the fearsome Yankees.

Jack certainly leaves a positive impression on almost everyone he meets for the first time. After our initial face-to-face meeting/interview, I was completely amazed with his honesty and openness when answering my questions. There was something about him that made me feel comfortable, and welcomed to his domain in the visitors clubhouse at Shea Stadium. When I left, it seemed like we had known each other for years and now we're good friends.

I have interviewed hundreds of people over the years, and never came across a celebrity as down-to-earth and real, as Jack McKeon. He shoots from the hip, and is not afraid to tell it like it is. He has a tremendous sense of humor and is never short on good jokes or outstanding baseball stories from his long and highly successful career.

When it comes to public speaking, McKeon always captivates the audience, whether there are 10 or 10,000 people, and they all come away feeling better after being touched by his message. One of his favorite sayings, which he credits to Charlie Finley is, "When Mr. Opportunity knocks, open the door and let him in." Jack has done that throughout his life, and in 2003, his big break came along, when Mr. Opportunity called on the phone, and he was hired by the Marlins. He sure made the most of it, by leading and inspiring Florida to the World Series Championship!

Watching Jack engineer one of the biggest upsets in Major League Baseball history reminded me of the "Miracle Mets" of Gil Hodges in 1969, who also overcame all odds to rule the world of baseball.

McKeon certainly has paid his dues, over 50 years worth in pro ball, and along the way has touched countless lives with hope through his positive and uplifting philosophy. He has definitely made me a believer in many things, especially one of his favorite quotes, "Everyone has a dream, and dreams do come true." I'll be the first to admit that I am a disciple of Jack McKeon and very proud of it. He is the kind of role model that the youth of today really needs.

Jack McKeon: Baseball, Cigars & Saint Theresa is a book that is loaded with rare photos from his brilliant career; great quotes and stories about Jack from family, teammates and players past and present; many in-depth interviews with Jack as well as other famous people in the baseball world; and rare, full-length feature stories from *The South Amboy-Sayreville Times* newspaper. You can also test your knowledge about Jack McKeon and his colorful life in the Trivia section, in this insightful and most importantly, fun book. FUN happens to be one of Jack's favorite words, so enjoy it, and learn about the life and times of Jack McKeon, one of the most colorful and interesting men in the history of Major League Baseball.

The Early Days

1. Jack McKeon was born on?

    a. November 23, 1930
    b. July 3, 1941
    c. December 24, 1950

2. Where was Jack born?

    a. Charlotte, NC
    b. New Brunswick, NJ
    c. South Amboy, NJ

3. His real name is?

    a. John Joseph McKeon
    b. John Aloysius McKeon
    c. Jacob Patrick McKeon

4. Jack's birth order was?

    a. eldest of seven children
    b. youngest of three children
    c. eldest of four children

5. McKeon was raised as a?

    a. Catholic
    b. Protestant
    c. Methodist

Answers

1a 2c 3b 4c 5a

5

Now Catching, Number 66?

Sure sounds like a football number doesn't it? Well, in Jack's senior year at St. Mary's High School in 1948, the team got new uniforms, and you guessed it, the All-County catcher, Jack McKeon wore uniform number 66. The lowest number was 50. Numbers this high were unheard of on baseball uniforms back then.

6. As a youngster, his favorite team was?

    a. New York Yankees
    b. Brooklyn Dodgers
    c. New York Giants

7. He saw his first major league baseball game at?

    a. Yankee Stadium
    b. Ebbets Field
    c. The Polo Grounds

8. At his first major league baseball game in the 1940's, he caught a foul ball off the bat of?

    a. Joe DiMaggio
    b. Duke Snider
    c. Phil Rizzuto

9. His father never owned?

    a. a taxi company
    b. a pizza parlor
    c. a towing service

10. At 20 years old, Jack's dad was the youngest man in the country to own?

    a. an airline
    b. a Ford dealership
    c. a funeral parlor

Answers
6a 7a 8c 9b 10b

Jack Managed At 14 Years Old

Jack McKeon managed his first baseball team at the very young age of 14 years old. He remembers, "I booked the games through the newspaper, and my father had the transportation for us, so it was easy. I just assembled a group of guys from South Amboy and we played. We were pretty good."

Did You Know?

McKeon attended the same high school, (St. Mary's South Amboy) as former Minnesota Twins' manager Tom Kelly, whose teams won the World Series in 1987 and 1991, and Allie Clark, who was a member of the '47, New York Yankees, and the '48 Cleveland Indians, who both won the World Series.

The famous O'Brien twins, Johnny and Eddie also attended St. Mary's, and graduated with Jack in the Class of 1948. The O'Briens went on to star in baseball and basketball at Seattle University, and were the first "Bonus Babies" signed by the Pittsburgh Pirates in the early 1950's.

Eddie "Buddy" Popowski, of the neighboring town of Sayreville was with the Boston Red Sox organization for 64 years as a player, coach and manager. He was the third base coach for the great 1967 Bosox club that went to the World Series.

Allie Clark, Jack's Boyhood Hero

Allie Clark, played for two World Series Champions in his first two seasons in the majors, the New York Yankees in 1947, and the Cleveland Indians in 1948. He and one other player have the distinction of being the only players in baseball history to have accomplished this feat. Clark also played for the Philadelphia Athletics and Chicago White Sox.

Clark is from Jack McKeon's hometown of South Amboy, New Jersey, and Jack as a youngster idolized Allie Clark, and to this day always signals him out in his speeches for "Showing us the way, for being an inspiration."

The following is taken from an interview on June 21, 2004 at Allie's home in South Amboy:

Allie Clark

"Jackie's (Jack's) father had a taxi garage about a half block from where I lived, and that's where I'd see Jackie all the time when he was growing up. He was always playing ball as a young guy. Early in baseball, I took him up to the Newark Bears (Allie played for the Bears in the International League) to workout.

I was surprised when he signed with the Pirates. I thought maybe, because he worked out with the Newark Bears, the Yankees might of got a hold of him, but it was a good break for Jackie getting with Pittsburgh. I never saw him play, but they say he was a good catcher. I used to see him when he came home in the off season. I kept in touch with him mostly when I got out of baseball, when he was managing and a general manager. I used to go up and see him when he'd come into New York.

I remember Jack McKeon Day at Yankee Stadium. I was on the committee. He was with Kansas City at the time. There were about seven or eight of us that handled it. I had to present Jack with a little gift, and a couple of other people gave him something as an appreciation of him being there. A group from South Amboy honored Jack. It was a nice crowd and a great day. The weather was beautiful.

It was amazing when the Marlins hired him last year. He was retired, and when he got a chance like that, I imagine he was very happy. As you know, it all turned out beautiful! He did a great job!

I have three Yankee jackets and hats, and everybody asked me who I was rooting for in the World Series, and I said I'm rooting for Jackie and the Marlins because he's from my hometown, and he's a great guy, and the Yankees, well, I didn't wear a Yankee jacket or Yankee hat for three weeks. It turned out that Florida won. It was a great series because Jackie did a good job. He had a good pitching staff. Anytime you have good pitching, it beats good hitting."

When asked why McKeon has been so successful for over 50 years, Allie said, "I think the ballplayers like him. He's not harsh with them. I think he lets them do mostly what they want to do, and he gets along fine with them. He's not one of these guys that if something goes wrong with a ballplayer, to go up and chew them out in front of everybody. He'll take them in the office and give 'em hell over what they did wrong."

How does Allie feel about Jack always praising him and giving him credit for being his boyhood idol and inspiration?

"Well, it makes me feel wonderful! I was one of the first players to make it, and Jackie looked up to me, and I guess the rest of the ballplayers from South Amboy did. It means an awful lot to me. No matter where he goes and makes a speech, he mentions my name, and it makes me feel great!

Whenever he came into town, he made sure his sister got a hold of me, and we'd get together and talk for awhile. It made me feel great that he wanted to see me!"

We talked about the possibility of Jack making the Hall-of-Fame if he wins another World Series. Allie said, "It would be wonderful if he made it! A manager and fellow from our hometown of South Amboy making it. I think he might have a shot for all the years he put into baseball, and to win two World Series, two years in a row. He'll have a great shot. I think it'll make the whole town feel wonderful.

Allie spoke about his alma mater, St. Mary's High School having graduates that have won a combined five World Series rings. "I don't think there's a high school in the country that has five World Series winners out of one school, and five World Series rings from one school, and that is amazing! I'm surprised that the daily newspapers never mentioned that. I've never seen it in the paper. It was never brought up on TV during the World Series either."

Note: Clark has won two World Series rings, Tom Kelly won in 1987 and 1991 as manager of the Minnesota Twins, and McKeon in 2003 with the Marlins. It was a great accomplishment for a school in a mile-square town, and what is really surprising is the fact that none of the national TV sports shows mentioned it or did a story about this tremendous feat in a small town. It certainly would have been a most interesting story, especially during the 2003 World Series.

Allie Clark concluded the interview by saying, "I hope he wins the pennant again, gets to the World Series and wins that. I think after that, he'll retire to that chair he was sitting in when he got the call in 2003."

11. Jack's father served as?

    a. Justice Of The Peace
    b. Fire Chief
    c. Civil Defense Coordinator

12. As a teenager, Jack was?

    a. a Water Meter Reader
    b. a Special Policeman
    c. a Building Inspector

13. He occasionally filled in for?

    a. the mailman
    b. the insurance agent
    c. the fire marshal

Answers
11a 12b 13a

14. Jack's father encouraged him to invest in and open?

    a. a drive-in movie theater
    b. a laundromat
    c. a car wash

15. His father wanted him to become?

    a. a doctor
    b. a baseball player
    c. a funeral director

Did You Know?

Jack's high school graduating class in 1948 had only 58 students, 30 girls and 28 boys. It's amazing to note that three of the boys, McKeon and the O'Brien twins, Johnny and Eddie made it to the major leagues, and Ray Stockton, star pitcher of the team played minor league ball and once faced and struck out the great Mickey Mantle.

16. McKeon's uncle Ed was?

    a. Mayor
    b. Tax Collector
    c. Police Captain

17. How did Jack go to the prom?

    a. in a limousine
    b. in his taxi
    c. on his bus

18. McKeon was a substitute teacher for?

    a. History
    b. Physical Education
    c. Business

Answers
14b 15c 16c 17b 18b

19. What was the first organized baseball team he played for?

    a. McKeon Boys Club
    b. Flaming Tigers AC
    c. The Little Yankees

20. What high school did Jack attend?

    a. St. Benedict's Prep
    b. St. Mary's
    c. Harold G. Hoffman

The Power of Prayer

McKeon said that his father wouldn't let him sign a contract and play as a professional when he was a teenager. He wanted him to go to college, and Jack attended Holy Cross for awhile. He said he started praying to Saint Theresa so his father would change his mind, and finally he did.

Did You Know?

The first major league game Jack went to see as a youngster, featured the Yankees, and he caught a foul ball off the bat of Phil Rizzuto.

Jack Said:

(About getting publicity, good or bad)

"As somebody said, "as long as they get your name out there, and spell it right, who cares?"

21. Jack's favorite hangout was?

    a. the local ice cream parlor
    b. the diner
    c. the corner by the bank

Answers
19a 20b 21c

22. In high school he was nicknamed?

a. Buck
b. Buzz
c. Butts

23. Jack was a two-time All-State baseball player. What position did he play?

a. first base
b. catcher
c. third base

24. As a senior in 1948, he was an important member of the state championship team in this sport?

a. baseball
b. basketball
c. football

25. What position did Jack play on the basketball team?
a. guard
b. forward
c. backup center

26. This former major leaguer from McKeon's hometown would take him to workouts to catch batting practice for his minor league team in the late 1940's?

a. Allie Clark
b. Pete Pavich
c. Walt Rogers

27. What team did he workout with?

a. Jersey City Jerseys
b. Newark Bears
c. Somerset Patriots

Answers
22c 23b 24b 25a 26a 27b

28. Jack received a baseball scholarship to?

    a. Holy Cross
    b. Notre Dame
    c. North Carolina State

29. What team did not heavily scout the talented McKeon?

    a. Washington Senators
    b. Pittsburgh Pirates
    c. Boston Red Sox

30. Jack was signed to a professional contract by?
    a. New York Giants
    b. Pittsburgh Pirates
    c. Detroit Tigers

Answers
28a 29a 30b

Jack Said:

"If I wasn't in baseball, I would probably be in the teaching and coaching profession."

Jack Was A Champion As A Teenager

In 1946, 15-year old Jack McKeon was the star catcher for the South Amboy Goveagles, a team comprised of players from St. Mary's and Hoffman High Schools. The Goveagles went on to capture the Middlesex County Freeholders Junior Baseball Tournament, defeating Perth Amboy American Legion Post #45 by a score of 6-5 in 11 innings. Jack came through with the clutch, game-winning hit in this thriller.

McKeon then took it upon himself in the summer of '48 to organize a group of baseball players from both high schools. The club, known as the South Amboy All-Stars won the Middlesex County Freeholders Tournament, the New Jersey State Amateur Baseball Championship, and advanced to the National finals at Johnstown, Pennsylvania, before bowing to the defending champion, Washington, D.C.

"I put the team together, and we won the Freeholders Tournament, and then we played in the *Newark Star Ledger* Tournament for the right to go to Johnstown,

Pennsylvania. When we entered the Freeholders Tournament, we didn't realize that the winner got a chance to participate (In the state tournament), so we won that thing. That's when I said to Richie Ryan, (He was our high school baseball coach), 'Richie, you take over. It's too much for me.' So Richie came aboard and coached us in Johnstown."

McKeon Was Standout Catcher In 1948

In 1948, prior to the South Amboy All-Stars winning the New Jersey State Amateur Baseball Championship, a local daily newspaper ran the following article:

McKeon Big Factor In Team's Success

Another big factor in the All-Stars' march to the finals is the catching of Jack McKeon. "He has everything, a baseball brain, a good arm and handles pitchers well," said Coach Richie Ryan. In both tournaments, McKeon did not have a passed ball charged against him, and his debut in Newark convinced most of the opposition that attempted steals would be foolhardy.

Note: Jack's old teammate, Jerry Connors told us that Jack and Leo Kedzierski could not play in the All-Stars quarterfinal game, because of an obligation to compete in the semifinal game for the South Amboy A.A. (Men's League team) in the state tournament.

It wasn't easy, but the All-Stars won without Jack, 4-3, but South Amboy A.A. dropped a heartbreaking 1-0 contest. Jack was only 17 years old at the time and was the starting catcher for both the All-Stars, and the South Amboy A.A. men's team.

31. Jack was signed by this big league scout?

    a. Gene Thomas
    b. Billy Beavers
    c. Tom Greenwade

32. His contract called for?

    a. $215 per month, plus continued education
    b. $300 per month, plus a new car
    c. $410 per month, plus an off-season apartment

Answers
31a 32a

Military Service

33. Jack enlisted in what branch of the military?

    a. U.S. Marine Corps
    b. U.S. Air Force
    c. U.S. Army

34. When did he enlist?

    a. During World War II
    b. During the Korean War
    c. During the Cuban Crisis

35. Where was he assigned?

    a. Camp LeJune, NC
    b. Sampson, NY
    c. Fort Dix, NJ

36. While in the military he was?

    a. a military policeman
    b. a clerk
    c. in charge of intramural sports

37. His military service team won?

    a. The USMC Eastern championship
    b. The US Army World Series title
    c. The World Air Force championship

Answers
33b 34b 35b 36c 37c

Minor Leagues

38. His first professional club was?

a. Evansville, Indiana
b. Syracuse, New York
c. Greenville, Alabama

39. What level did they play at?

a. Class A ball
b. Rookie League
c. Class D ball

40. His first roommate on the professional level was?

a. Evan Law (brother of pitching great, Vernon Law)
b. Mario Cuomo (who became Governor of New York)
c. Roberto Clemente

41. Jack's first professional manager was?

a. Honus Wagner
b. Walter Tauscher
c. Danny Murtaugh

42. How did the team finish?
a. won the pennant
b. second place
c. tied for last

43. Where did Jack spend his first spring training as a professional?

a. Havana, Cuba
b. New Orleans
c. Daytona Beach, Florida

Did You Know?

McKeon won his first championship ring in 1949, as an 18-year old catcher for Greenville, Alabama Pirates. The team captured the Alabama State League title in a thrilling finish. With 12 games left, and trailing by six, they won 12 in a row to cop the championship. Jack said "the ring was a flat piece of gold."

44. How much did McKeon weigh at the start of the '49 season?

    a. 200 pounds
    b. 235 pounds
    c. 254 pounds

45. At the end of the season, he weighed?

    a. 175 pounds
    b. 193 pounds
    c. 204 pounds

46. He led all catchers in?

    a. assists
    b. putouts and double plays
    c. passed balls and errors

47. Jack also topped the league in?

    a. batting average
    b. fielding average
    c. hits

Answers
44b 45c 46b 47b

Durable Catcher

McKeon was a durable catcher in the Pittsburgh Pirates farm system, catching in 139 of the Burlington team's 140 games in 1953. He also played in the other game, too. Jack led catchers in virtually every defensive category.

Jack Said:

(On his big break in managing)

"I think Branch Rickey was the first person to recognize my talents and give me a chance to manage."

48. In 1950, he reported in weighing?

  a. 172 pounds
  b. 195 pounds
  c. 201 pounds

49. In 1950, he was originally assigned to the York Red Roses in Class B ball, but was reassigned to?

  a. Class B, Charleston
  b. Class C, Gloversville, NY
  c. Class AA, Toledo

50. How much was he paid monthly in '50?

  a. $165
  b. $195
  c. $225

51. In the 1950's, he told Pittsburgh Pirates owner, Branch Rickey that Jack McKeon would make a good manager?

  a. Gabby Hartnett
  b. Paul Waner
  c. Danny Murtaugh

52. After his discharge from the Air Force, he played for?

  a. Topeka, Kansas
  b. Hutchinson, Kansas
  c. Selma, Alabama

Answers
48a 49b 50c 51c 52b

18

Someone Was Watching Him In 1950

In 1950, while catching for Gloversville in Class C ball, Jack injured his ankle, and the team wanted to send him home to South Amboy, New Jersey for a rest. He decided to hang around until Sunday, and it's a good thing he did. If he had left when they asked, he would have pulled into the South Amboy Train Station, two minutes before the munitions explosion in May, 1950. Many people were killed and injured, and the town looked like a war zone. Someone up there was watching young Jack McKeon on that day.

53. How much did GM, Dick Wagner pay him at Hutchinson in '53?

  a. $225 per month
  b. $3,000 per year
  c. $237.50 per month

54. Jack's manager at Burlington was?

  a. Mickey Cochrane
  b. George Selkirk
  c. Wes Griffin

55. In 1953 while playing for Burlington, North Carolina in Class B ball, what did Jack do for the first time?

  a. started chewing tobacco
  b. began switch-hitting
  c. blasted four home runs in one game

56. This legendary owner asked Jack to manage the Clinton, Iowa team in 1954?
  a. Connie Mack
  b. Bill Veeck
  c. Branch Rickey

57. How old was Jack when he started managing in the minor leagues?
  a. 24
  b. 30
  c. 34

Answers
53c 54c 55b 56c 57a

Jack Fact:

On June 11, 1955, the 24-year old, McKeon was named player/manager of Fayetteville (NC). It was his first professional managing opportunity, and he took advantage of it, and had the club in a first place tie, but on August 6, a hand injury forced him out of the lineup, and management replaced him in a budgetary move that allowed one person to handle both jobs.

Jack Said:

(When asked what his favorite town was to play in as a minor leaguer)

"Every town I ever played in was a favorite to me, as long as I could put the uniform on."

58. What was the first professional team he ever managed?

a. Des Moines, IA
b. South Bend, IN
c. Fayetteville, NC

59. As manager of Appleton, Wisconsin in 1959, he had a talented shortstop, who would go on to become the American League MVP in '65?

a. Luis Aparicio
b. Zoilo Versalles
c. Maury Wills

60. While managing at Missoula, he had his first base coach, Gene Curtis lasso this player with a clothesline to keep him from taking too big of a lead?

a. Rod Carew
b. Sandy Valdespino
c. Caesar Tovar

Jack Fact:

His best offensive season as a minor league player was in 1958, when he batted .263 for Missoula of the Pioneer League.

Answers
58c 59b 60b

61. This future Minnesota Twins' great got his start pitching for McKeon at Missoula?

   a. Jim Perry
   b. Jim Kaat
   c. Jim "Mudcat" Grant

62. Jack was player/manager at Missoula from 1956-1958. Besides catching, what position did he play?

   a. first base
   b. right field
   c. pitcher

63. In 1958, with Missoula, he had his highest batting average. What was it?

   a. .263
   b. .285
   c. .304

64. While managing at Wilson, North Carolina, he once "shot" this player with a blank gun for running through his stop sign at third base?

   a. Chico Carrasqual
   b. Floyd Robinson
   c. Juan Visteur

65. He pitched for McKeon at Wilson, and later became the Minnesota Twins farm director?

   a. Camilio Pascual
   b. Jim Rantz
   c. Jim Kaat

Answers
61b 62c 63a 64c 65b

21

66. In the minors, Jack once decked this opposing player, who became a big league manager?

a. Tony LaRussa
b. Doc Edwards
c. Dave Johnson

67. Burlington newspapers once called Jack?

a. Rocky
b. Ingemar
c. Killer

Jack Said:

(On when he pitched in the minor leagues)

"We had a 17-man roster with seven or eight pitchers, and I'd come in the game and mop up, when we were getting beat 9-1 or 10-1. I'd go in and pitch, and save my pitchers for tomorrow. I had a great ERA. I had my "Atom Pitch." I just threw a batting practice pitch, and they hit it right at 'em."

68. How did the '61 Wilson team fare in the Carolina League under Jack's tutelage?

a. they won the pennant
b. second place
c. they finished dead last

69. Wilson was an affiliate of what big league club?

a. Minnesota Twins
b. Philadelphia Athletics
c. Milwaukee Braves

70. In '62, he was promoted to this Triple-A team?

a. Richmond Braves
b. Tacoma Twisters
c. Vancouver Mounties

Answers
66b 67b 68a 69a 70c

71. One of his coaches in '62 was?

    a. Roger Craig
    b. George Bamberger
    c. Dallas Green

72. Jack always had a creative mind, and while at Triple-A, he became the first manager to?

    a. use the radar gun on pitchers
    b. have a pitcher wired with a transmitter and receiver
    c. use orange colored baseballs

Jack The Talent Scout

In the 1960's, while serving as Special Assignment Scout for the Minnesota Twins, McKeon recommended that they draft Steve Garvey. The Twins listened to Jack's advice, but Garvey opted for college.

73. Who was the first player used with McKeon's invention?

    a. Jerry Arrigo
    b. Dick Stigman
    c. George Bamberger

74. When Denver players hit a home run, the scoreboard at Mile High Stadium would explode. In answer to that, when Jack's players hit a home run, he?

    a. lit up sparklers and waved them around
    b. shot blank guns into the air
    c. set off firecrackers

75. In '64 he managed this Triple-A team?

    a. Rochester Red Wings
    b. Tacoma Twins
    c. Atlanta Crackers

Answers
71b 72b 73c 74b 75c

76. The team's winning percentage was?

    a. .311
    b. .500
    c. .605

77. He managed Winter League ball in the off-season for six years in this country?

    a. Venezuela
    b. Dominican Republic
    c. Puerto Rico

Jack The Beatle?

The Beatles took America by storm in 1964, and all you would see on the news or read in the paper was about the Fab Four, John, Paul, Ringo and George. There was no Jack, or was there? Well, just for one game at Columbus, when Jack McKeon wore a Beatles wig when he exchanged lineup cards at home plate. The crowd roared its approval for the always entertaining manager.

78. What Triple-A club did McKeon manage in 1969 and 1970?

    a. Tidewater
    b. Omaha
    c. Dallas-Fort Worth

79. What team was the parent club?

    a. Kansas City Royals
    b. Milwaukee Brewers
    c. Seattle Pilots

80. How did his 1969 and 1970 clubs fare?

    a. won two pennants
    b. one first place finish, one second place
    c. won the pennant in '69 and came in third in '70

Answers
76a 77c 78b 79a 80a

81. He caught for Jack's club in 1970, and went on to become an outstanding sportscaster?

a. Fran Healy
b. Buck Martinez
c. Bob Uecker

82. He was Jack's pitching coach on the '70 team?

a. Bob Friend
b. Galen Cisco
c. Pedro Ramos

Jack Predicted

Jack McKeon managed pitcher Steve Busby at Omaha in 1972. McKeon recalled, "In one game, Steve had a no-hitter going into the ninth before it was broken up. When that happened, I went to the mound and told him to forget about it, that he'd get it in the major leagues. Now you see what I meant." He meant that Busby certainly did get his no-hitter with the Kansas City Royals, on April 27, 1973, a 3-0 masterpiece against the Detroit Tigers.

83. He broadcast the games played by Jack's team in 1969 and 1970?

a. Bill Beck
b. Curt Gowdy
c. Harry Cary

84. He once managed this club during the winter in Puerto Rico?

a. Santurce
b. Ponce
c. Arecibo

85. In '76, he managed this Triple-A club?

a. Greenville
b. Richmond
c. Ogden

Answers
81a 82b 83a 84c 85b

86. Who's farm system was it?

   a. Atlanta
   b. Chicago Cubs
   c. Cincinnati

87. In 1976, while at this Triple-A team, he managed this future home run slugger?

   a. Jose Canseco
   b. Dale Murphy
   c. Dave Kingman

Jack Fact:

   In 17 seasons as a minor league manager, he compiled a record of 1146-1123, a .505 winning percentage. He was named Manager of the Year four times: 1958 at Missoula of the Pioneer League, 1961 at Wilson of the Carolina League and two straight awards in the American Association, with Omaha in both 1969 and 1970.

88. In '79, McKeon managed his last minor league team. Where?

   a. Richmond
   b. Tacoma
   c. Denver

89. What team won 85 games for Jack in the minor leagues? This was the most victories by any of his clubs in the minors?

   a. 1962 Vancouver
   b. 1964 Atlanta
   c. 1969 Omaha

Answers
86a 87b 88c 89c

1969-Jack (l), manager of Omaha in the American Association and his brother Bill (r), the scouting supervisor. Jack took the Triple A club to two consecutive league titles in 1969-70, and was chosen "Manager of The Year" both seasons. (Photo courtesy of Bill McKeon)

Kansas City Royals

90. This Kansas City owner gave McKeon his first major league manager's job?

    a. Ray Kroc
    b. Horace Stoneham
    c. Ewing Kauffman

91. What was Jack's rookie year as manager of the Kansas City Royals?

    a. 1969
    b. 1973
    c. 1976

92. What was the team's record under its new skipper?

    a. 81-81
    b. 88-74
    c. 90-72

Answers
90c 91b 92b

93. What place did Jack guide the Royals to in his rookie year?

a. first
b. second
c. third

94. Who did McKeon replace as manager?

a. Bob Lemon
b. Dick Williams
c. Chuck Tanner

Did You Know?

In 1973, as rookie manager of the Kansas City Royals, McKeon finished a solid second place in the Associated Press' Manager of the Year Award voting to Earl Weaver of Baltimore. Jack's 91 votes were 50 ahead of third place finisher, Dick Williams.

95. What uniform number did he wear in '73?

a. 8
b. 10
c. 31

96. How much was he paid in his first year with the Royals?

a. $20,000
b. $25,000
c. $30,000

97. During his managing days at Kansas City, McKeon had a house in?

a. Kansas City
b. Topeka
c. Independence

Answers
93b 94a 95c 96c 97c

98. In 1973, Jack's hometown held a day for him at?

a. Yankee Stadium
b. Veterans Stadium
c. Royals Stadium

99. Approximately how many people from Jack's hometown attended the game?

a. 500
b. 2,500
c. 6,000

1973-South Amboy's Tom Ryan organized "Jack McKeon Day" at Yankee Stadium to honor the Kansas City Royals rookie manager. Pictured (l-r) Thomas English, Mayor of Madison Twp., N.J., Jack, Allie Clark and Tom Ryan. (Photo courtesy of Tom Ryan)

Answers
98a 99a

"Jack McKeon Day"
At Yankee Stadium Recalled By Organizer Tom Ryan

Tom Ryan, a well-respected South Amboy, N.J. businessman for over 36 years and owner of Sure Hit Home Improvements, has been a friend of Jack McKeon's family for most of his life.

Back in 1973, when he found out that Jack was hired to manage the Kansas City Royals in the major leagues, he decided it was time to hold a day to honor him at Yankee Stadium.

Ryan said, "We had some memorabilia on "Allie Clark Day" that South Amboy gave him at Yankee Stadium in 1948, and felt that we should do the same for Jack for his great accomplishment. I talked to my wife Shirley and said, 'Let's get together and see if we can have a "Jack McKeon Day." Then I called the City Fathers, and they called the Madison Township Mayor, and we got together and began planning. We called different businesses for gifts, and also tried to get a car, but that didn't work out. We advertised in the newspapers and all over to sell tickets, and I think we got 18 bus loads going up that day.

It was a nice day. We had a good turnout, and the stadium was quite full. I remember everybody making presentations, and when it was my turn, I handed Jack his gift, shook his hand, and was ready to talk in the microphone, at this big event at Yankee Stadium, and a plane flew over and drowned me out. So my big speech was downplayed by the plane. Everybody smiled.

Jack took us around the stadium and into the clubhouse, and we met John Mayberry and a few other players. It was a great day!

"Jack McKeon Day" was way up there, one of the five top events in my life. I was a friend of his mother and father, and when you personally know somebody in that position, and as it turned out, he became a great manager. In the beginning, he just plain managed, and that in itself was an accomplishment. Now, he turned out to be a super-manager, so he's way up there. It's just a nice feeling that I know him."

Ryan also recalled the good old days in South Amboy. "Jack's father had an Amoco station by Christ Church Cemetery and we used to buy our gas there. We were only kids, and would hang out there. Jack was never around much because he was always playing baseball in the minors and managing. I was good friends with his brother "Biff" and sister Marge. I once said to Jack that out of all the people that ever played baseball, through all the years, and there's only one manager per team. The odds of becoming a manager were so great to be one of many, many. He said he never thought of it that way."

100. In '73, he battled the front office to get this player promoted?

a. Willie Wilson
b. Amos Otis
c. Frank White

101. How many second place clubs did Jack manage at Kansas City?

a. one
b. two
c. four

102. In 1973, this sportscaster did a feature on national TV, "The Life of A Rookie Manager" about Jack McKeon?

a. Mel Allen
b. Joe Garagiola
c. Tony Kubek

103. He led Jack's '73 Royals in runs (89), hits (175), batting average (.300), and tied for the home run lead with (26)?

a. Lou Piniella
b. Amos Otis
c. John Mayberry

104. His 28 doubles topped Kansas City in 1973?

a. Cookie Rojas
b. Lou Piniella
c. Ed Kirkpatrick

Jack Said:

(In 1973 as manager of the Royals)

"All the individual numbers in the world don't mean a thing unless the team plays well. I like to make things happen. I don't believe in a lot of that stereotype, traditional stuff in baseball. I do ask the players to play for the team. I want the Royals to become known as the smartest team in baseball."

105. This player hit five triples and stole 36 bases to lead manager McKeon's 1973 Royals?

    a. Paul Schaal
    b. Freddie Patek
    c. Gail Hopkins

106. He was the ace of the '73 Royals' pitching staff, as he topped the team with (20) wins, and (262) innings pitched?

    a. Paul Splittorff
    b. Steve Busby
    c. Dick Drago

107. This pitcher struck out 174 batters to lead Kansas City for Jack McKeon in '73?

    a. Al Fitzmorris
    b. Bruce Dal Canton
    c. Steve Busby

108. He notched 20 saves, the high mark for the 1973 Royals?

    a. Gene Garber
    b. Doug Bird
    c. Joe Hoerner

109. How much did his contract call for in 1974?
    a. $32,000
    b. $34,000
    c. $35,000

Answers
105b 106a 107c 108b 109c

Jack Said:

"The thing I learned when I managed the Royals was that you gotta be part manager, part psychiatrist."

110. He was not one of McKeon's coaches on the Royals in '74?

    a. Charlie Lau
    b. Galen Cisco
    c. Hal McRae

111. What place did Kansas City finish in 1974?

    a. second
    b. fifth
    c. last

112. Ewing Kaufmann, Royals owner once gave Jack a reward. What was it?

    a. a new Chevy pickup truck
    b. a motel in Kansas City
    c. 100 shares in his development company

113. In '74, Jack wanted to replace one of his coaches and hire?

    a. Steve Boros
    b. Rico Petrocelli
    c. Clete Boyer

114. He led the Royals in four major offensive categories in 1974: Hits (167), doubles (36), and RBI (88), and batting average (.310)?

    a. Amos Otis
    b. Hal McRae
    c. George Brett

Answers
110c 111b 112c 113a 114b

1965-67-Jack scouted for the Minnesota Twins.
(Photo courtesy of Bill McKeon)

1965-Jack (l) scouted for the Minnesota Twins, and his brother Bill (r) was a Los Angeles Dodgers scout. This photo was taken during the World Series between the Twins and Dodgers, which was won by LA.
(Photo courtesy of Bill McKeon)

George Brett Said:

(In 2004)

"Jack was my first manager in the big leagues, and I'm happy for his success."

115. He blasted 22 home runs to top McKeon's '74 Kansas City Royals?

a. Vada Pinson
b. Fran Healy
c. John Mayberry

116. The ace pitcher of McKeon's staff with (22 wins), (292 innings), and (198) strikeouts in '74 was?

a. Al Fitzmorris
b. Paul Splittorff
c. Steve Busby

117. How much was Jack paid in 1975?

a. $40,000
b. $45,000
c. $50,000

118. Jack was fired as manager in '75 and replaced by?

a. Gene Mauch
b. Whitey Herzog
c. Ralph Houk

119. Jack's '73 Royals set a team record for?

a. lowest ERA
b. most hits
c. most home runs

120. In 1974, they set a club record against Minnesota by scoring?

a. 15 runs
b. 18 runs
c. 23 runs

A Long Trip To The Big Show

(Excerpted from an interview at Shea Stadium in September 2003)

I asked Jack, 'Why do you think it took so long for you to become a major league manager?' McKeon answered, "The timing. Showing people you could do it at the minor league level, and having a sponsor-someone who takes a liking to you, in my case Mr. Kauffman of the Kansas City club. I did well in the minors, and he liked the way I went about my work. He felt it was time for me to come to the big leagues."

1961-McKeon led Wilson to the Carolina League championship, and was chosen "Manager of The Year."

Oakland Athletics

121. In late '75 Jack joined the Oakland organization as an?

    a. Advance Scout
    b. Third Base Coach
    c. Assistant to the President

122. This legendary and eccentric owner hired McKeon to manage his Oakland Athletics?

    a. Buzzy Bavasi
    b. Charles Finley
    c. Gene Autry

123. In '77, Jack succeeded him as manager of the Oakland Athletics?

    a. Billy Martin
    b. Chuck Tanner
    c. Dick Williams

124. How much did the A's pay McKeon in 1977?

    a. $30,000
    b. $40,000
    c. $45,000

125. What was McKeon's uniform number with the A's?

    a. 1
    b. 3
    c. 31

Answers
121a 122b 123b 124c 125a

Jack Almost Got Guidry

When managing the Oakland A's, Jack said that in Spring Training, he had a deal ready which would send Mitchell Page to the New York Yankees for Ron Guidry. Eccentric owner, Charles O. Finley stopped the deal. Could you imagine the "Gator" in the Kelly green and gold of the A's?

126. Who was Jack's pitching coach in '77?

    a. Milt Pappas
    b. Lee Stange
    c. Harvey Haddix

127. One of his other coaches in 1977 was?

    a. Harry Chiti
    b. Elio Chacon
    c. Red Schoendienst

128. Jack was fired on June 10, 1977. He was replaced by?

    a. Bobby Winkles
    b. Larry Dierker
    c. Bill Virdon

129. At the time of his firing, the A's record was?

    a. 27-26
    b. 26-27
    c. 20-33

130. He started the '78 season with the A's as?

    a. an advance scout
    b. general manager
    c. a coach

Answers
126b 127c 128a 129b 130c

By The Numbers

McKeon was the first Oakland Athletics manager to wear uniform number 1. Bobby Winkles and Billy Martin later wore number 1.

Jack's uniform number was #15 while at the helm of the San Diego Padres.

131. In 1978, he was rehired to replace?

    a. Bobby Winkles
    b. Tony LaRussa
    c. Herman Franks

132. Just out of high school, this A's top draft pick pitched for Jack in the big leagues?

    a. Ray Burris
    b. Mike Morgan
    c. Ken Holtzman

133. The A's #2 draft pick, also a 17-year old out of high school pitched for McKeon.   What was his name?

    a. Tim Conroy
    b. Vida Blue
    c. John "Blue Moon" Odom

134. Jack's overall won-lost record at Oakland was?

    a. 71-105
    b. 75-101
    c. 88-88

135. In '79, he became the A's manager, replacing Jack McKeon?

    a. Jim Marshall
    b. Hank Bauer
    c. Gene Tenace

Answers
131a 132b 133a 134a 135a

1940-Jack's father, Bill was a well-respected businessman in New Jersey. Here he is shown driving South Amboy's Mayoral candidate, John Zdanewicz (hatless) during a parade. (Photo courtesy of Marge Gorczyca)

1943-The McKeon Boys Club, organized by Jack's father was the first ball club he played on. Five of the boys went on to pro become pros. Pictured top row (l-r) Stan Kowaleski, "Peanuts" Leonard, Ray Stockton, Art Sullivan, Art Jensen; 2nd row (l-r) Murphy, unknown, Jack McKeon; 3rd row (l-r) John O'Brien, Bill McKeon, Joe Seminaro, Ed O'Brien, Joe Lovely, Jim Rea, Dan Noble; front row (l-r) "Bud" Larkin, Jim McKeon-mascot, "Chinky" Koziak. Missing from photo is Coach Chet Meinzer Sr. (Photo courtesy of Marge Gorczyca)

1947-McKeon, a rugged rebounder and tenacious defender, started as a guard on the St. Mary's '48 Catholic School State Champions. (Photo courtesy of Marge Gorczyca)

Jack's boyhood idol, Allie Clark, who played for the 1947 World Champion New York Yankees. (Photo courtesy of Allie Clark)

1947-48-The legendary St. Mary's High School basketball powerhouse that went on to capture the state title. Pictured top (l-r) Gene Harkins, Joe Servon, Jerry Hoban, Joe Kress, Jack McKeon, Jerry Connors; middle row (l-r) John "King" Larkin, Alfie O'Connor, Ed O'Brien, Coach Reggie Carney Sr., John O'Brien, Frank Carney; bottom (l-r) Jack O'Toole, Jack Vail, Ray Stockton, Bob "Ace" Hennessey, Adam Lovely-mascot. (Photo courtesy of Ed O'Brien)

1948-Jack (r) wearing his letterman's sweater is shown with old friend, Jim Hanaway (l) who was home on leave from the service. (Photo courtesy of Ceil Gosford)

1948-St. Mary's talented baseball team that sent six players to professional baseball. Top row (l-r) Ray Stockton, Art Sullivan, John Higgins, Jerry Connors, John Larkin, Jack Vail, Bill McKeon, Ed O'Brien, Jerry Hoban,. Bottom row (l-r) Jack McKeon, Vince Abbatiello, John O'Brien, Bob Kenny, Mascot "Lefty" Dadon, Alfie O'Connor, Bill Creed, Bob Hennessey, Archangelo DiMattia.

1948-The South Amboy All-Stars baseball squad that went on to capture the New State Amateur Baseball championship. Pictured top row (l-r) Coach Rich Ryan, Jim O'Brien, Bill McKeon, Jack McKeon, John Skarzynski, Leo Kedzierski, Ray Wisniewski, John Larkin, Jack Zawacki, Ed O'Brien, Assistant Coach, Bill Ryan; bottom row (l-r) Bob Kenny, John O'Brien, Al O'Connor, Bob Hennessey, John Kovaleski, Ray Stockton. (Photo courtesy of Ed O'Brien)

1948-Pictured at the NJ Amateur Baseball Tournament are (l-r) Joe Jerome, Jack McKeon, Jack's father Bill, Bill McKeon. (Photo courtesy of Marge Gorczyca)

1948-17-year old Jack McKeon (r) was catching in the South Amboy City League. Pitcher, Stanley Kusic (l) celebrates with his battery mate after another victory.
(Photo courtesy of Stanley Kusic)

1950-McKeon was the first-string catcher
for Gloversville.
(Photo courtesy of Bill McKeon)

1951-As a 20-year old player/manager,
he led Sampson (NY) Air Force Base to
the Air Force championship.
(Photo courtesy of Marge Gorczyca)

45

1952-The Hutchinson Elks team consisted of : Standing (l-r) Bob Flynn, Mat Kuhn, Bill Wiltrout, Jack O'Keefe, Art Murray, Bob Anderton, Jack Brown, Rex Babcock, Gerry Collins, Frank Washington.   Seated (l-r) Bob Prescott, Whitey Cline, Lee Beran, Steve Butchko, Jack Quinn, Bob Denny, Jack McKeon, Manager Wes Griffin.

1956-The second professional team that Jack managed was the Missoula Timberjacks in the Pioneer League. Standing (l-r) Bennie Sinquefield, Aaron Jones, Joe Abernathy, Tom Yankus, Clay Bryant, Chuck Weatherspoon, Dal Womack, Don Schneider.   Middle row (l-r) Player/Manager, Jack McKeon, Espinoza, Jack Vandersee, Dick Schultz, Al Viotto, Jack O'Laughlin, Reno Barbisan. Sitting (l-r) Dave, batboy, Frank Schulz, clubhouse boy.
(Photo courtesy of Dick Schultz)

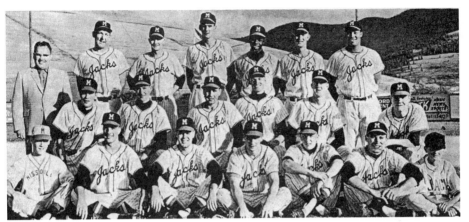

1957-The Missoula Timberjacks team competed in the Pioneer League. Front Row (l-r) Frank Schulz clubhouse boy; Tom Palamar of; Dick Schultz p; Don Dantoni ss; Addie Hintze 2b; Jim Russell p-of; Jeff Herman bat boy. Middle Row (l-r) Mike Hiney 3b; Wayne Tucker 1b; Jack McKeon c-manager; Larry Foss p; Billy Sheffield p; Gene Curtiss p. Back Row (l-r) Nick Mariana, president-GM; Dick Greco lf; Bennie Sinquefield cf; Earl Furlow p; Chuck Weatherspoon c-of; Tony Tegenkamp; Aaron Jones p. (Photo courtesy of Dick Schultz)

Jack managed the San Diego Padres from 1988-1990.

Jack returns to dugout after a trip to the mound.
(Photo courtesy of Cincinnati Reds)

Hall of Fame catcher, Johnny Bench (r) visits
with McKeon prior to a Reds game.
(Photo courtesy of the Cincinnati Reds)

Number 31 pauses by Reds dugout at Cinergy Field.

2000-Jack goes over the finer points of the game with star first baseman, Sean Casey during batting practice in late September.

The Unpredictable Charlie Finley

Oakland A's owner, Charles O. Finley, known for his whims and unpredictability, hired and fired the same manager three different times. Feeling the axe and wrath of Finley were Alvin Dark, Hank Bauer and Jack McKeon.

Jack Said:

(On A's eccentric owner, Charlie Finley)

"When he hired me, he said he was the owner, general manager and part-time manager."

Jack Fact

While with Charlie Finley and the Oakland Athletics, McKeon held various positions, including assistant general manager, scouting director, manager, scout and coach.

McKeon Had Hope

(When hired to manage the Oakland Athletics in 1977)

"I think it's great. We can patch this thing up and turn the club around in spite of all the players we've lost. I like to try to make things happen, and maybe we can surprise some people again."

Did You Know?

When Jack managed the Oakland A's, team owner Charlie Finley once sent him a case of Geritol to give to his star player, Dick Allen.

Dick Allen's Arrival At Oakland

The Oakland A's acquired controversial Dick Allen, and owner Charlie Finley told manager Jack McKeon to personally pick him up at the airport. McKeon also had to set up a press conference.

The next day, Jack put him in as the DH, and Allen said, "I ain't DH'ing. It's in my contract with Finley." McKeon said, "I had to pinch hit for him in the first inning."

San Diego Padres

136. This person was not an owner of the Padres?

   a. Ballard Smith
   b. Ray Kroc
   c. Joan Kroc

137. What year did McKeon start working for San Diego as a Scout/Assistant to the GM?

   a. 1977
   b. 1978
   c. 1980

138. Jack said the day the Padres won the pennant was the day they acquired this player from the New York Yankees?

   a. Goose Gossage
   b. Jerry Mumphrey
   c. Graig Nettles

139. This big league owner sent McKeon a congratulatory telegram when the Padres clinched the pennant?

   a. George Steinbrenner
   b. Charles O. Finley
   c. Bill Veeck

140. Jack received this famous nickname for making many blockbuster trades as GM of the Padres?

   a. Wheeler Dealer
   b. Trader Jack
   c. Make A Deal McKeon

Trader Jack's First Trade

Jack McKeon engineered his first of some 45 trades as Vice President/ Baseball Operations with the San Diego Padres in 1980. The four-player exchange sent Mark Lee and Kurt Bevacqua to Pittsburgh for Rick Lancellotti and Luis Salazar.

Did You Know?

Although Jack became famous for his nickname, "Trader Jack," he had another less-known moniker while with San Diego. He was also called, "The Sultan of Swap."

141. He was GM Jack's manager of the '84 Padres?

    a. Tommy LaSorda
    b. Dick Williams
    c. Jim Frey

142. The 1984, NL Champs finished with a record of?

    a. 100-62
    b. 92-70
    c. 95-67

143. His biggest trade was an 11-player blockbuster deal that involved this Hall-of- Famer?

    a. Tony Gwynn
    b. Rollie Fingers
    c. Steve Garvey

144. In '87, McKeon hired him for his first big league managing job with the Padres?

    a. Clint Hurdle
    b. Larry Bowa
    c. Joe Altobelli

Answers
141b 142b 143b 144b

Did You Know?

That after the 1984 San Diego Padres won the National League pennant, Jack received a telegram from New York Yankees owner, George Steinbrenner. The message read: "The lions share of the credit has to go to you. You were patient. You made some great moves. You took me to the cleaners. And I am happy for you. You should be very proud of the job you did. Sincerely, George Steinbrenner."

145. In 1988, Jack was named manager of San Diego by this club president?

a. Horace Stoneham
b. Lee Thomas
c. Chub Feeney

146. Who did McKeon replace as manager?

a. Don Zimmer
b. Jim Leyland
c. Larry Bowa

147. What years did he manage San Diego?

a. 1983-86
b. 1988-90
c. 1991-94

148. In '88, he held two titles with the Padres. What were they?

a. assistant to the owner/GM
b. manager/vice president of baseball operations
c. advance scout/VP special acquisitions

149. In '88 after taking over the club, he guided them to a record of?

a. 56-56
b. 60-52
c. 67-48

Answers
145c 146c 147b 148b 149c

150. From when he took over, the team rose from last place to?

a. first
b. second
c. third

151. What place did McKeon finish in the balloting for Manager of the Year in *The Sporting News*, and with the BBWAA in 1988?

a. second
b. fourth
c. fifth

152. On September 14, 1988, the Padres rewarded him with a contract for how long?

a. two years
b. three years
c. five years

153. Who was Jack's good friend that was the Padres Director of Media Relations in 1988?

a. Danny Ozark
b. Bill Beck
c. Johnny Miller

154. This talented rookie started and starred for McKeon's Padres in '88?

a. Roberto Alomar
b. Benito Santiago
c. Bip Roberts

155. How many games did the Padres win in 1989 under McKeon?

a. 75
b. 84
c. 89

Did You Know?

McKeon became manager of the San Diego Padres on May 28, 1988. His son-in-law, Greg Booker, a pitcher for the club had appeared in 17 of the Padres first 46 games. He pitched in only 17 more games the rest of the season.

156. What place did his '89 Padres finish?

a. second
b. third
c. last

157. In 1989, he topped San Diego with a (.336) average, (203) hits, and tied for the lead in runs and doubles.

a. Tony Gwynn
b. Roberto Alomar
c. Gary Templeton

158. He led the '89 Padres in RBI (94) and home runs (26)?

a. Steve Garvey
b. Jack Clark
c. Chris James

159. The Padres' stolen base champ with (42) in 1989 was?

a. Gary Templeton
b. Luis Salazar
c. Roberto Alomar

160. This pitcher topped San Diego with 16 wins in '89?

a. Eric Show
b. Walt Terrell
c. Ed Whitson

Did You Know?

Jack spotted speedster, Alan Wiggins with Lodi, a Los Angeles Dodgers farm club, where he stole 120 bases. McKeon saw him swipe second, third, and home, twice in the same game, and was convinced San Diego could use him. Wiggins was drafted by San Diego for $25,000 in December 1980.

161. He paced McKeon's pitching staff in '89 with (245) innings, and (179) strikeouts?

a. Ed Whitson
b. Bruce Hurst
c. Dennis Rasmussen

162. This pitcher notched 44 saves in route to winning the 1989 NL Cy Young Award?

a. Greg Harris
b. Mark Davis
c. Mark Grant

163. After a 37-43 start in 1990, he was replaced as manager by?

a. Dick Williams
b. Greg Riddoch
c. Joe Altobelli

164. McKeon once traded this outstanding player?

a. Steve Garvey
b. Tony Gwynn
c. Ozzie Smith

165. How many second place finishers did Jack bring in at San Diego?

a. none
b. one
c. two

Answers
161b 162b 163b 164c 165b

Did You Know?

In 1988, Sandy Alomar Sr. was McKeon's third base coach on the San Diego Padres. In '89, Pat Dobson was his pitching coach.

166. His career record with the Padres was?

    a. 190-167
    b. 193-164
    c. 200-157

167. While at San Diego, Jack was voluntarily involved with a baseball league for?

    a. disabled children
    b. alcoholics
    c. orphans

168. Approximately how many trades did Jack complete while with San Diego?

    a. 13
    b. 29
    c. 45

169. In 1989, he traded his son-in-law, Greg Booker, a pitcher to Minnesota for?

    a. Gary Gaetti
    b. Randy Bush
    c. Fred Toliver

170. In 1990, Jack resigned as Padres' manager, but retained this position until September 21?

    a. vice president of baseball operations
    b. assistant to the president
    c. director of operations

Answers
166b 167a 168c 169c 170a

57

171. How many years was Jack away from managing, when he was named skipper of San Diego?

a. two
b. five
c. nine

Did You Know?

When the Padres were trying to trade for Graig Nettles, Owner, George Steinbrenner did not want to deal with GM McKeon.

According to McKeon in his book, *Jack of All Trades*, "Steinbrenner apparently felt I'd taken advantage of him in the Mumphrey deal. So he refused to negotiate the Nettles deal directly with me. He said he would only talk to Ballard, (Smith, Padres President), and I really didn't give a hoot. Because when Ballard was speaking on the phone with George, I was sitting in a chair right next to Ballard. I told him exactly what to say and what to do, and who to ask for."

Jack Said:

On getting third baseman, Graig Nettles from the Yankees, "In my opinion, the day we acquired Nettles was the day we won the pennant."

3-Year Contract For McKeon

After the 1988 baseball season, the San Diego Padres signed Jack to a 3-year contract for a reported $1.2 million.

Dark Day In Padres History

July 11, 1990-Jack McKeon resigned as manager of the San Diego Padres, but kept his position as Vice President of Baseball Operations. He was replaced in the dugout by Greg Riddoch.

Answer
171c

Cincinnati Reds

172. Jack served in this position from 1993-1997 with the Reds?

   a. Assistant to the General Manager
   b. General Manager
   c. Senior Adviser for Player Personnel

173. Who was the Cincinnati Reds' owner who hired Jack to manage the club?

   a. Bob Howsam
   b. John Quinn
   c. Marge Schott

174. Jack was named manager of the Reds in?

   a. 1993
   b. 1997
   c. 1999

175. Who did he succeed as manager of Cincinnati?

   a. Ray Knight
   b. Dave Johnson
   c. Lou Piniella

176. What was the team's record under McKeon that season?

   a. 30-33
   b. 31-32
   c. 33-30

Jack Said:

(At the end of the '99 season)

"The team overachieved all year, everybody had career years. That may not happen next year, and guess whose fault it will be? Mine. So I want a two-year contract."

Answers
172c 173c 174b 175a 176c

177. During that 63 game span in '97, the Reds' record was?

    a. the best in the National League
    b. second best in the NL East
    c. the best in the NL Central

178. What years did he manage Cincinnati?

    a. 1993-95
    b. 1996-97
    c. 1997-2000

179. What was Cincinnati's record under McKeon in '98?

    a. 77-85
    b. 81-81
    c. 90-62

180. What uniform number did he wear in 1998?

    a. 7
    b. 10
    c. 15

181. The Reds' GM during McKeon's stay was?

    a. Brian Cashman
    b. Jim Bowden
    c. Walt Jocketty

Jack Said:

(On his team's many injuries throughout the 2000 season)
"We've got more MRI's than RBI's on this team.

182. In 1999, he led Cincinnati to a record of?

    a. 100-62
    b. 96-67
    c. 90-72

183. The Pitching Coach for McKeon at Cincinnati was?

    a. Milt Pappas
    b. Dave Righetti
    c. Don Gullett

184. McKeon utilized him as Bullpen Catcher for the Reds?

    a. Gene Oliver
    b. Mark Berry
    c. Clarence "Choo Choo Coleman

185. The '99 Reds lost a one-game playoff to?

    a. St. Louis Cardinals
    b. Atlanta Braves
    c. New York Mets

186. What did Jack do radio and TV commercials for while at Cincinnati?

    a. a new car company
    b. a cigar company
    c. stereo systems

Answers
182b 183c 184b 185c 186b

187. The Hitting Instructor for McKeon's Reds in 2000?

a. Denis Menke
b. Rick Monday
c. Wally Moon

188. What prestigious Associated Press award did McKeon win in '99?

a. Manager of The Year
b. Fred Hutchinson Award
c. The Hickock Belt

189. After his outstanding, award-winning year in 1999, the Reds extended his contract for another year, and gave him a paltry raise of?

a. $33,000
b. $45,000
c. $50,000

190. He served as McKeon's bullpen coach with Cincy?

a. Tom Hume
b. Diego Segui
c. Wes Stock

191. What uniform number did he wear while with the Reds in 1999 and 2000?

a. 1
b. 31
c. 44

192. The Reds fired Jack at the end of 2000 after the team finished?

a. second place
b. fourth place
c. last place

Answers
187a 188a 189a 190a 191b 192a

193. How many Cincinnati teams finished second place under McKeon?

    a. one
    b. two
    c. three

194. In 1999, he became the first Reds' manager in history to win this BBWAA award?

    a. Man of The Year
    b. National League Manager of The Year
    c. Sportsman of The Year

195. In '99, he won this prestigious award?

    a. Associated Press Manager of The Year
    b. Cincinnati Man of The Year
    c. BBWAA Good Guy

196. In 1999, he finished second in the balloting for Manager of The Year in *The Sporting News.* Who won?

    a. Tony LaRussa
    b. Bobby Cox
    c. Bobby Valentine

197. He served as the Reds first base coach under Jack McKeon?

    a. George Foster
    b. Dave Collins
    c. Robin Yount

Did You Know?

In 1999, Jack became the third manager in Reds history to win the Associated Press' Manager of the Year Award. Fred Hutchinson won the award in 1961, and Sparky Anderson took the honor in 1972 and 1975.

Answers
193b 194b 195a 196b 197b

198. What was their record in 2000?

    a. 81-81
    b. 85-77
    c. 90-72

199. Who succeeded Jack as manager of the Reds?

    a. Ron Oester
    b. Bob Boone
    c. Tony Perez

200. McKeon's longtime coach, who was with him at Kansas City in '74, and also an Instructor at Cincinnati?

    a. Harry Dunlop
    b. Cookie Rojas
    c. Frank Crosetti

201. He was third base coach for McKeon with the Reds?

    a. Ron Oester
    b. Dave Concepcion
    c. Paul Molitor

202. McKeon's Bench Coach with Cincy was?

    a. Vada Pinson
    b. John McNamara
    c. Ken Griffey Sr.

Did You Know?

Jack McKeon 's record with the Cincinnati Reds in two-plus seasons was 291-259, a winning percentage of .529. The victories place him at number 9 on the Reds' all-time list.

Answers
198b 199b 200a 201a 202c

64

Favorite Places

Jack's favorite places to manage as of August 2002 were San Diego and Cincinnati. (We're pretty sure that Florida is now his favorite). He said, "I enjoyed managing at San Diego and Cincinnati." Of course, both teams had winning years. "The only one I had a bad year with was Oakland. We had a bad team," he said.

Jack piloted the Cincinnati Reds from 1997-2000. (Photo courtesy of Cincinnati Reds)

McKeon has always been a fan favorite.

Florida Marlins

203. McKeon took over the reins of manager of the Florida Marlins on?

    a. Memorial Day
    b. Mother's Day
    c. The Fourth of July

204. Jack's first game with the Marlins was a 7-2 victory over?

    a. Pittsburgh
    b. Colorado
    c. St. Louis

205. What was Florida's record when Jack became manager?

    a. 22-16
    b. 19-19
    c. 16-22

206. Who did Jack succeed as Marlins' manager?

    a. Jim Leyland
    b. Rene Lachemann
    c. Jeff Torborg

207. The 2003 season marked how many years for McKeon as a manager in the major leagues?

    a. 10
    b. 12
    c. 13

208. How many managers were there in Florida Marlins' history before Jack signed on?

    a. two
    b. four
    c. six

Answers
203b 204b 205c 206c 207c 208c

The Big Call-May 10, 2003

On the night of May 10, 2003, Jack McKeon was relaxing at home in Elon, North Carolina watching the Cleveland Indians-Texas Rangers game on his satellite dish, of course smoking his favorite cigar. The phone rang at 10:45 p.m., and it was Larry Beinfest, General Manager of the Florida Marlins asking Jack to become the manager of the club, and the rest is history!

209. What other manager besides McKeon led the Marlins to the World Series title?

a. John Boles
b. Tony Perez
c. Jim Leyland

210. How old was Jack McKeon when he took over the helm of the Florida Marlins?

a. 69
b. 72
c. 77

211. In Major League Baseball history, McKeon became the?

a. oldest manager
b. the second oldest manager
c. the third oldest manager

212. Who is the Marlins' owner who hired Jack despite his age?

a. Jeffrey Loria
b. Carl Pohlad
c. George Steinbrenner

213. A good friend of McKeon's helped him to get the interview for the manager's job. Who was it?

a. John Boggs
b. Rich Mullaney
c. Bill Beck

Answers
209c 210b 211c 212a 213c

67

Did You Know?

When Jack won his inaugural game with Florida, it was his 771st career victory. That's great, but consider it was 48 more wins than the Marlins notched in the 11-year history of the franchise.

214. This GM was instrumental in bringing McKeon to Florida?

a. Larry Beinfest
b. Joe Garagiola, Jr.
c. Omar Minaya

215. Where did McKeon live during the 2003 baseball season?

a. in a motel
b. in his sister's condo
c. in a rented house

216. What town did Jack reside in during the 2003 season?

a. Miami
b. Deerfield Beach
c. Hallandale Beach

217. During the season, this player's mother sent a bouquet of roses to McKeon in appreciation for what he had done for the Florida Marlins?

a. Josh Beckett
b. Andy Fox
c. Todd Hollandsworth

Jack Said:

(On his first meeting with the Marlins after taking over as manager)
"I told them I didn't need the job, that I didn't need my ego stroked. I told them I was here to help make them better players and a better team. There's enough talent in this room if you want to work. You've done it your way, now do it my way. I want to be playing in October."

Answers
214a 215b 216c 217a

218. What is his uniform number?

 a. 11
 b. 13
 c. 15

219. He was McKeon's third base coach in 2003?

 a. Jack Clark
 b. Ozzie Guillen
 c. Matt Galante

220. The bullpen coach for McKeon's Marlins in '03 was?

 a. Jeff Cox
 b. Paul Splittorff
 c. Jake Gibbs

221. The 2003 hitting coach for the Marlins?

 a. Jim Rice
 b. Bill Robinson
 c. Mike Easler

222. McKeon's pitching coach in '03 was?

 a. Wayne Rosenthal
 b. Dave Righetti
 c. Bill Monboquette

Did You Know?

When McKeon made his managerial debut in 1973 with the Kansas City Royals, only 10 of the 2003 Florida Marlins players had been born.

Jack Said:

(On age)

"Age doesn't mean a thing. Age is just a number. I don't think of myself as old. I don't feel old."

Answers
218c 219b 220a 221b 222a

223. Florida's first base coach in 2003 was?

    a. Willie Randolph
    b. Perry Hill
    c. Jose Cruz Sr.

224. McKeon's bench coach on the World Champion Marlins was?

    a. Doug Davis
    b. Harry Dunlop
    c. Don Zimmer

225. Jack felt that this club ran up the score on the Marlins in a regular season game?

    a. Atlanta Braves
    b. Boston Red Sox
    c. Philadelphia Phillies

226. McKeon's Marlins' three game sweep over this team clinched a tie for the Wild Card spot?

    a. Colorado Rockies
    b. Milwaukee Brewers
    c. Philadelphia Phillies

227. Florida won the Wild Card playoff spot by beating this club?

    a. New York Mets
    b. St. Louis Cardinals
    c. Los Angeles Dodgers

Jack Said:

(On stealing bases)
"We try to pick the important times to run, crucial times in the game. They all have the green light to steal."

Answers
223b 224a 225b 226c 227a

Jack On The Cubs

(During the World Series)

"The Cubs were always America's favorites, and now I think we're the darlings of the baseball world."

228. This club battled the Marlins' for the Wild Card slot?

    a. Philadelphia Phillies
    b. New York Mets
    c. Pittsburgh Pirates

229. Under McKeon, Florida finished 75-49, .605, which was?

    a. the best percentage in Marlins' history
    b. second best record in the club's history
    c. tied for third best record in team history

230. This youngster won the National League Rookie-of-The-Year Award for 2003, while blossoming under skipper McKeon?

    a. Juan Pierre
    b. Miguel Cabrera
    c. Dontrelle Willis

231. Jack McKeon's speedster who was the major league's stolen base king in 2003?

    a. Luis Castillo
    b. Alex Gonzalez
    c. Juan Pierre

232. Prior to McKeon and the Marlins, how many managers guided their teams to a playoff berth after taking over in mid-season?

    a. one
    b. six
    c. eleven

Answers
228a 229a 230c 231c 232c

Jack Said

(On his Florida Players)

"What makes a good manager is good players, and these guys have done the job."

Did You Know?

After the 2003 season, Jack had the highest lifetime winning percentage, .605 in Florida Marlins history.

233. The last manager, prior to Jack to lead his club to the playoffs after taking over in mid-season was?

   a. Bill Russell
   b. Cito Gaston
   c. Dick Howser

234. In the NL playoffs, this broadcaster, who formerly played for Jack, heaped lots of praise on his old manager?

   a. George Brett
   b. Tony Gwynn
   c. Al Leiter

235. The Marlins, with McKeon guiding them breezed to a 3-1 NLDS series win over?

   a. San Francisco Giants
   b. Houston Astros
   c. Atlanta Braves

236. Florida defeated the Chicago Cubs to win the National League Championship Series in how many games?

   a. five
   b. six
   c. seven

Answers
233a 234b 235a 236c

237. During a celebration with Florida fans, what did Jack do?

a. sang "The Star Spangled Banner
b. played drums
c. danced to "Twist and Shout"

Jack Said:

(When the 2003 playoffs began)
"The pressure is on everybody else, because we aren't supposed to win."

238. How many games did it take for McKeon's Miracle Marlins to defeat the Yankees and win the World Series Championship?

a. four
b. five
c. six

239. Jack intentionally walked this superstar many times in post season, and his strategy paid off? Who was this power hitter?

a. Sammy Sosa
b. Barry Bonds
c. Jason Giambi

240. Throughout the post season, TV cameras showed McKeon in the dugout chewing and spitting?

a. tobacco
b. pumpkin seeds
c. sunflower seeds

241. He played for McKeon at Cincinnati, and against him with the Yankees in the World Series?

a. Paul O'Neill
b. Jeff Nelson
c. Aaron Boone

Answers
237b 238c 239b 240c 241c

242. As the crowd gave Roger Clemens a standing ovation after being taken out in what was believed to be his final game, what did McKeon do?

a. waved and smiled
b. went over and shook Clemens' hand
c. tipped his hat towards Clemens

Jack Said:

(On the 2003 Marlins)
"This is the most selfless major league team I've ever managed."

Jack Said:

(In August 2002)
In an interview when Jack was between jobs, he spoke about who he thought would be in the World Series. He said, "It's pretty tough to compete against the Yankees."

Little did he know then, that a year later, Jack "The Giant Slayer" and his Florida Marlins would shock the baseball world, by beating the mighty Yankees in six games to capture the World Series championship.

243. Jack's controversial gamble to start this pitcher in Game 6 after only three days rest, paid huge dividends and brought the World Championship to the Florida Marlins?

a. Carl Pavano
b. Josh Beckett
c. Dontrelle Willis

244. The biggest controversy surrounding Jack during the post-season was?

a. Josh Beckett pitching on three days rest
b. benching Juan Encarnacion
c. moving Miguel Cabrera to right field

Answers
242c 243b 244a

74

245. What did the Marlins' players do after the final out of the World Series?

    a. piled on Jack McKeon
    b. knelt down in group prayer
    c. hoisted Jack McKeon on their shoulders

246. Before Game 5 of the World Series, McKeon received this gift from the Marlins' owner for reaching the World Series?

    a. a 50-foot yacht
    b. two race horses
    c. a new Mercedes sports car

247. Where was the gift waiting for Jack?

    a. at a private yacht club in Miami
    b. in the parking lot at Pro Player Stadium
    c. in a stable at the Gulfstream Racetrack

Jack Said:

(About Cub fan Steve Bartman, who deflected a ball in the NLCS)

"I feel sorry for the way they are crucifying that guy. People forget the shortstop bobbled the next ball and we scored seven runs. They (Cub fans) don't want to give the Marlins credit for being a resilient club."

Did You Know?

Jack McKeon is believed to be the oldest coach or manager hired in any of the four major sports.

248. McKeon became only the second manager to win a World Series after not beginning the season with his club. Who was the first?

    a. Billy Martin
    b. Bob Lemon
    c. Harry Craft

Answers
245c 246c 247b 248b

249. By winning the World Series, McKeon became?

   a. The oldest in baseball history to win the World Series
   b. The second oldest to win the World Series
   c. Tied for the second oldest to win the World Series

250. A Florida daily newspaper called Jack this name after winning the World Series?
   a. Mr. Miracle
   b. Grandpa Miracle
   c. Gambler Jack

251. What did Jack do in New York with just two hours of sleep, the morning after winning the World Series?

   a. helped out serving in a soup kitchen in Harlem
   b. attended Mass
   c. went to the Empire State Building

Answers
249a 250b 251b

Money Didn't Buy The World Series Crown

The New York Yankees estimated payroll for 2003 was $183 million, compared to the Florida Marlins, which was only $54 million. Guess you can't always buy the World Series Championship.

Jack gives the thumbs-up sign prior to Game 2 of the World Series at Yankee Stadium. Unfortunately, the Marlins lost the game, but bounced back to capture the World Series championship over the heavily-favored Yankees.

Jack Said:

(On the Yankees and Joe Torre)
"The Yanks and Joe Torre scared the hell out of us."

Off Season 2003, Early 2004

252. Florida held two parades for the Marlins. This town did not have a parade?

a. Fort Lauderdale
b. Miami
c. Sarasota

253. When did the owner announce that McKeon would return to manage in 2004?

a. at a costume party on Halloween
b. during the team's World Series celebration party
c. at the post-game press conference in Yankee Stadium

254. Jack's signed a 2004 contract extension for a reported?

a. $900,000
b. $1 million
c. $1.5 million

255. Who re-negotiated the new contract?

a. Joshua Rubenstein
b. Jack McKeon
c. John Boggs

256. How long did the meeting for the new contract take?

a. four hours
b. one day
c. three days

Answers
252c 253b 254a 255b 256a

Jack Said:

(On his new contract)

"I just wanted to come back and see if we couldn't do it again. Whatever players they give me, I'll do the best I can."

257. What national TV talk show did Jack appear on?

a. Jay Lenno
b. Late Night With David Letterman
c. Oprah Winfrey

258. Jack served as Grand Marshal of the Christmas Parade at?

a. Burlington, North Carolina
b. Miami Beach, Florida
c. Missoula, Montana

259. Jack and another person were selected "Sportsmen of The Year" for 2003 by?

a. Sport Magazine
b. Sporting News
c. Sports Weekly

260. Who shared the honor with Jack?

a. Brett Favre
b. Dick Vermeil
c. Phil Jackson

261. McKeon's photo was featured on a cover overleaf in this national publication?

a. Baseball Digest
b. Sports Illustrated
c. Recreational Sports

Answers
257b 258a 259b 260b 261b

78

Jack Said:

(On leadoff hitter Juan Pierre)

"He jump starts our offense. People overlook what kind of clutch hitter he is. He's a very detailed person. He's out here at one o'clock rolling balls down the first base line, checking the grass, throwing balls against the wall to check the caroms. He really wants to be good. I wish everyone in the game had his drive."

262. Who shared the cover overleaf with him on *Sports Illustrated*?

a. Carmelo Anthony
b. Kobe Bryant
c. Shaquille O'Neal

263. Who presented Jack with the 2003 National League "Manager of The Year" Award at the Baseball Writers Association of America Dinner on January 25, 2004?

a. Tony Pena
b. Art Howe
c. Joe Torre

264. Where was the event held?

a. Chicago
b. Miami
c. New York

265. In his acceptance speech, McKeon mentioned one current player. Who was it?

a. Roger Clemens
b. Josh Beckett
c. Barry Bonds

Answers
262a 263b 264c 265a

266. Who finished 2nd place behind Jack for 2003 NL Manager of the Year?"

    a. Felipe Alou
    b. Dusty Baker
    c. Bobby Cox

267. Who did the Marlins' sign as bullpen coach for 2004?

    a. Mel Stottlemyre
    b. Tony Taylor
    c. Cesar Cedeno

268. What did Jack and the Marlins do as team in early 2004?

    a. Went on a cruise to the Bahamas
    b. Went to the White House to meet President Bush
    c. Took a weekend trip to Las Vegas

Answers
266b 267b 268b

Did You Know?

Two of Jack's favorite opposing managers are Bruce Bochy and Tommy LaSorda.

Jack McKeon is pictured at the White House in Washington, D.C. on January 23, 2004.

Family

269. What was Jack's father's name?
   a. William
   b. John
   c. Patrick

270. Jack' wife is named?

   a. Carol
   b. Karen
   c. Bonnie

271. What is her maiden name?

   a. O'Brien
   b. Isley
   c. Jones

272. Where did he meet his wife?

   a. at a church picnic
   b. at the beach
   c. at a ballgame

273. Where did his wife grow up?

   a. Little Rock, Arkansas
   b. Burlington, North Carolina
   c. Elon, North Carolina

Answers
269a 270a 271b 272c 273b

Jack Talks About His Father

In his first book, *Jack of All Trades*, McKeon talked about his dad, William who died in December 1966.

"My father meant so much to me. All my street smarts I got from him, all my get up and go. He's the reason I went anywhere in life."

274. How many children do Jack and his wife have?

a. two
b. four
c. seven

275. All of their children's first names begin with the same initial. What is it?

a. "J"
b. "C"
c. "K"

276. Jack's oldest son is?

a. Roger
b. Kasey
c. Kelly

277. McKeon has two daughters named?

a. Joan and Janice
b. Kristi and Kori
c. Colleen and Cherise

278. Which one of Jack's children and their family lives right next door to him?

a. Kasey
b. Kristi
c. Kelly

Baseball Babies

Jack and Carol's daughter Kristi was born on the day his Wilson team won the Carolina League championship in 1960. Their son Kelly was born on the date that Wilson clinched the title in 1961.

Answers
274b 275c 276c 277b 278b

279. How many grandchildren do Jack and Carol have?

    a. five
    b. seven
    c. nine

280. His brother's name is?

    a. Bill
    b. Bob
    c. Brett

281. His brother's nickname is?

    a. Bronco
    b. Biff
    c. B.J.

282. McKeon's brother was?

    a. a conductor on a train
    b. a baseball player
    c. a chef

283. In high school, Jack's brother was an All-State baseball player at this position?

    a. pitcher
    b. center field
    c. catcher

284. Jack's sister is one of his biggest fans. Her name is?

    a. Marge
    b. Joan
    c. June

Answers
279c 280a 281b 282b 283c 284a

285. McKeon's sister is a highly energized and organized person just like him. She is affectionately known by this nickname?

    a. Commander
    b. The General
    c. Napoleon

286. Jack's son Kasey starred in baseball at this college?

    a. North Carolina State
    b. Rutgers University
    c. San Diego State

287. Jack's son Kasey played in the minor leagues. What position?

    a. catcher
    b. second base
    c. right field

288. What organization did Kasey play for?

    a. San Diego
    b. White Sox
    c. Detroit

289. Jack's son-in-law, Greg Booker pitched in the majors, and later worked for the San Diego Padres as an?

    a. advance scout
    b. pitching coach
    c. media relations specialist

Did You Know?

Jack once joked that all of his children's first names began with the letter "K" because K means strikeout, and he struck out a lot when he played.

Answers
285b 286c 287a 288c 289b

Potpourri

290. In 1949, McKeon experienced a first in his life. What was it?

  a. his first plane ride
  b. his first time in a Pullman (train)
  c. the first time he went hunting

291. Another first for Jack in that awakening year of '49 was?

  a. the first time he went surfing
  b. when he smoked his first cigar
  c. when he visited Alaska

292. Where does McKeon reside?

  a. Elon, North Carolina
  b. South Amboy, New Jersey
  c. San Diego, California

293. What is the population of the town which he resides in?

  a. 300
  b. 4,233
  c. 7,000

294. While at college, he became friends with this Athletic Director, baseball and basketball coach?

  a. Bear Bryant
  b. Doc Mathis
  c. John Wooden

Did You Know?

Every day when McKeon goes to daily Mass, he leaves a lit cigar by the door, and picks it up after the service is over.

Answers
290b 291b 292a 293c 294b

The Reds skipper thrills youngsters by signing autographs prior to a game against the Mets.

The Reds skipper chats with fans before game time.

2000-Two of Jack's right arm men with the Reds were instructor Harry Dunlop (l) and pitching coach, Don Gullett (r).

McKeon congratulates Sean Casey after a big Reds win. Pitcher Denny Neagle is number 15, and Travis "Gookie" Dawkins is number 6. (Courtesy of the Cincinnati Reds)

Jack waves to fans during batting practice at Shea Stadium.

Hall of Fame pitcher, Gaylord Perry (l) visited his old buddy Jack in late September 2000 at Cinergy Field in Cincinnati.

Reds' talented first baseman, Sean Casey (l) and McKeon (r) before an exhibition game at Sarasota, Florida during Spring Training 2000.

1999-Reds' broadcaster, Joe Nuxhall (r), who was the youngest player in Major League history (15), scopes the Cincy talent with McKeon (l). (Photo courtesy of the Cincinnati Reds)

Early 1980's-Smokey The Bear gets help from San Diego Padres' Vice President of Baseball Operations, Jack McKeon (r). McKeon asked the San Diego community to "help Smokey have a winning season. Don't be careless with fire"

Johnny and Ed O'Brien grew up in the same town as Jack McKeon. They played on the same teams with him from youth league through high school, and other clubs including the 1948 New Jersey Amateur Baseball champions. The O'Brien's were signed by the Pittsburgh Pirates after All-American careers at Seattle University. They were the most famous twins in the United States throughout the early 1950's. (Photo courtesy of Ed & Johnny O'Brien)

90

*The McKeon Family is pictured in this photo from the 1970's. (l-r) Jack,
his mother Anna, sister Kathy, brother Bill, and (foreground) sister Marge.
(Photo courtesy of Marge Gorczyca)*

*February 2000-Jack returned to South Amboy for "Jack McKeon Day," in which he
was honored by the city for his great accomplishments.*

*Jack was a featured guest signer at a Card Show/Fundraiser for
the South Amboy First Aid on February 5, 2000.*

*Anthony (l) and Victoria LaVigne (c) proudly show their baseballs which were
freshly autographed by their hero, Jack McKeon (r) at a Card Show/Fundraiser
for the South Amboy First Aid on February 5, 2000.*

2000-The South Amboy Knights of Columbus Council No. 426 pose proudly with their homegrown hero, Jack McKeon (front center) after the gala event, "An Evening With Jack McKeon," which featured a dinner and awards presentation at the K of C Hall.

South Amboy's Mayor John T. O'Leary presented McKeon with a Proclamation from the Mayor and City Council proclaiming February 5, 2000 "Jack McKeon Day" in the City of South Amboy.

Jack and his grandson, Kellan McKeon, pose for a great photo during a break in the action at Spring Training 2000 in Sarasota, Florida.

Jack McKeon (l) and Tom Kelly (r) got together before being inducted into their old high school's new Hall of Fame in 2000. Kelly who graduated in 1968 from St. Mary's went on to guide the Minnesota Twins to two World Series titles in 1987 and 1991. McKeon, a '48 grad, took the Florida Marlins to the top of the baseball world by winning the 2003 World Series.

Rare Photo-St. Mary's High School of South Amboy, New Jersey, in a town of one square mile, produced five major leaguers. Pictured together for the first time are (l-r) Ed O'Brien, Allie Clark, Jack McKeon, John O'Brien and Tom Kelly. The event marked St. Mary's High School's inaugural Hall of Fame induction in 2000.

Reds award-winning radio broadcaster, Marty Brennaman (r) and McKeon go over Cincinnati's progress during pre-game workouts. (Photo courtesy of the Cincinnati Reds)

295. Jack is a '63 graduate of this college?

    a. Elon College
    b. St. John's University
    c. North Carolina State

296. He received his Bachelor of Science degree in?

    a. Business Administration
    b. Accounting
    c. Physical Education

297. McKeon never attended this school of higher learning?

    a. Seton Hall University
    b. Holy Cross University
    c. Kansas State

298. As a Minnesota scout, he told the Twins to draft this New Jersey youngster?

    a. Steve Braun
    b. Tom Kelly
    c. Glenn Borgmann

299. McKeon's first deal was?

    a. when he sold his father's Amoco gas station for $30,000
    b. when he traded his coach for a player in the minors in '57
    c. when he traded Kevin McReynolds to the New York Mets

Did You Know?

That *Cigar Aficionado* magazine ran an excellent feature story on Jack McKeon in early 2004?

Answers
295a 296c 297c 298a 299a

300. Where did Jack manage in the winter of '75?

a. Mexico
b. Puerto Rico
c. Dominican Republic

301. Jack once had a tobacco spitting contest with this celebrity?

a. Burt Reynolds
b. Doc Severinson
c. Johnny Cash

302. McKeon said that one of his favorite people in baseball was?

a. Alan Wiggins
b. Paul Splittorff
c. Darrell Porter

303. This player met Jack McKeon for the first time at the Kansas City Royals Baseball Academy in 1973?

a. Reggie Jackson
b. Jeff Cox
c. Ozzie Smith

304. How many major league teams has he managed?

a. three
b. four
c. five

Did You Know?

In 1999, McKeon was honored by The New Jersey Sportswriters Association, and received both the Manager of the Year Award and the Distinguished Service to Baseball Award.

Answers
300b 301b 302b 303b 304c

305. In '77, he asked Jack to become his assistant?

    a. Ted Turner
    b. Gene Autry
    c. Bill Veeck

306. Jack never worked for?

    a. Marge Schott
    b. George Steinbrenner
    c. Charlie Finley

307. He served as a scout from 1965-67 with this club?

    a. Oakland Athletics
    b. Minnesota Twins
    c. Cincinnati Reds

308. While scouting, he worked for this owner?

    a. Calvin Griffith
    b. Marge Schott
    c. Charles O. Finley

309. After McKeon's first meeting with Marlins' Owner, Jeffrey Loria, he called him?

    a. Jimmy
    b. Jerry
    c. Jeffrey

Did You Know?

In 2003, he received the Manager of the Year Award and Man of the Year Award from the New Jersey Sportswriters Association.

Answers
305a 306b 307b 308a 309b

310. Former Twins manager Tom Kelly, and Jack McKeon both graduated from the same high school. What pitcher played for both Kelly at Minnesota, and Jack in Florida?

a. Ron Villone
b. Mark Redman
c. Braden Looper

311. This pitcher also played for McKeon at Cincinnati, and Kelly at Minnesota?

a. Mark Portugal
b. Pete Harnisch
c. Willie Banks

312. Jack had the same player four different times in his career. Who?

a. Kurt Bevacqua
b. Gary Templeton
c. Harmon Killebrew

313. McKeon traded this young player while he was GM of San Diego, and in 2003, the player was one of his coaches with the Florida Marlins?

a. Bill Robinson
b. Jeff Cox
c. Ozzie Guillen

314. What player did not pitch for Jack McKeon at San Diego, and later for Tom Kelly with the Minnesota Twins?

a. Eric Show
b. Greg Booker
c. Fred Toliver

"Barter" Jack

Following the '53 minor league baseball season, Jack met "Doc" Mathis, Athletic Director at Elon College, and helped him officiate baseball and basketball games in exchange for free tuition. Although it was about 25 years before the real "Trader Jack" began making ultimate trades for the San Diego Padres, Jack's ability to make a deal was always there.

One For The Books

Jack finished his college courses in 1957 at Elon College, but could not attend the graduation ceremony because of his baseball commitments, and did not receive a diploma until 1963.

315. Which one of Jack's sons is a Special Assistant to the General Manager, Dan O'Dowd of the Colorado Rockies?

   a. Kasey
   b. Carney
   c. Kelly

316. What other two teams did the same son once scout for?

   a. Padres and Royals
   b. Indians and Reds
   c. Marlins and Orioles

317. Jack's son scouted and signed?

   a. Dmitri Young
   b. Sean Casey
   c. Jim Thome

318. Jack once called this player "One of the greatest kids I'd ever seen?"

   a. Tony Gwynn
   b. Ozzie Smith
   c. Barry Bonds

Answers
315a 316b 317b 318a

100

319. Jack's agent is?

a. John Boggs
b. Alan Hendricks
c. Johnny Conley

All In The Family

In 1984, Jack and the San Diego Padres drafted his nephew, Kevin Gorczyca, a catcher, in the 19th Round of the Amateur Draft. Kevin, who starred for Hoffman High School in South Amboy, New Jersey, decided on a different career field.

320. One of McKeon's favorite players once saved his sister Kathy from drowning in a pool. Who was this lifesaver?

a. Steve Garvey
b. Chuck Weatherspoon
c. Tim Flannery

321. McKeon graduated from the same high school as this New York Mets Fox TV sportscaster?

a. Matt Loughlin
b. Tom Seaver
c. Ralph Kiner

322. Jack once interviewed for the GM job with this team?

a. New York Yankees
b. Baltimore Orioles
c. Milwaukee Braves

323. Jack never received a congratulatory telegram from this president?

a. John F. Kennedy
b. Richard M. Nixon
c. George H. W. Bush

Answers
319a 320b 321a 322b 323a

324. One of Jack's daily routines in the morning, no matter where his team is playing?

    a. is breakfast with three eggs over easy and three slices of French toast
    b. is attending Mass
    c. is talking a solo walk in the park

Man of Many Jobs

Jack has been in pro baseball for well-over 50 years, and has held all types of jobs in his profession. Most people would be surprised to find out some of the other non-baseball occupations he's worked at in his lifetime.

The diversified list includes: taxi driver, school bus driver, wrecker driver, gas station attendant, hosiery mill worker, mechanic, and he served in the U.S. Air Force. It's an almost definite that there were many other jobs, but this is a pretty interesting assortment, don't you think?

325. What did Jack buy his wife for their 49th Anniversary?

    a. a new car
    b. a ring
    c. a trip to Europe

326. One of McKeon's favorite house chores is?

    a. taking the garbage out
    b. cutting the grass
    c. grocery shopping

327. Jack was very successful with this diet in 2003?

    a. Atkins Diet
    b. South Beach
    c. Grapefruit

Did You Know?

In 13 major league seasons as manager, McKeon has produced six second place finishers (including one Wild Card), and a World Series Champion.

Answers
324b 325b 326b 327a

328. His favorite restaurant in Florida?

    a. Mandingo's
    b. Vito's
    c. Manero's

329. What two things does McKeon always carry in the back pocket of his uniform?

    a. a pen-knife and tiny flashlight
    b. a crucifix and rosary beads
    c. a rabbit's foot and lucky silver dollar

Jack's First Book

McKeon wrote his first book, a biography with Tom Friend in 1988. The book was appropriately titled *Jack of All Trades*.

330. Jack's favorite cigars are?

    a. Arturo Fuente and Padron
    b. White Owls and Visente
    c. Octobre and Havanas

331. What kind of mower does he use to cut the grass?

    a. a Cub Cadet riding mower
    b. a Snapper self-propelled
    c. a Toro riding tractor

332. In 2003, what picture did Jack have in his office near his desk?

    a. his family
    b. Saint Theresa
    c. President Bush

Answers
328c 329b 330a 331a 332b

333. Jack's good friend and superb sportscaster on ESPN's College Basketball is?

a. Tim McCarver
b. Chip Caray
c. Dick Vitale

334. Jack's wife Carol cuts the front lawn of their home. What does she use?

a. a John Deere tractor
b. a Snapper riding mower
c. a Craftsmen riding mower

The Good Guys

Jack McKeon once said that some of his favorite people in baseball were: Hall-of-Famer Harmon Killebrew, Paul Splittorff, Tony Solaita and Amos Otis.

Jack The Jokester

McKeon, one of the great comedians in the world of baseball, tossed this original joke at sportswriters one day: "So many people want to make something of my age. Well, I'm so old, I can remember Preparation A."

335. What year did he make Elon, North Carolina his permanent residence?

a. 1957
b. 1973
c. 1992

336. What is McKeon's favorite baseball movie?

a. The Natural
b. The Pride of The Yankees
c. Fear Strikes Out

Award Winner

In 1998, Jack was selected "Distinguished Alumnus of The Year" at Elon College.

Answers
333c 334a 335c 336b

337. One of McKeon's favorite sportscasters is?

    a. Fran Healy
    b. Harold Reynolds
    c. Rob Dibble

338. One of his favorite holiday songs is?

    a. Silver Bells
    b. White Christmas
    c. Deck The Halls

339. At Christmas time, his family has a?

    a. pine tree
    b. spruce tree
    c. artificial tree

340. What Zodiac sign is Jack born under?

    a. Aquarius
    b. Scorpio
    c. Sagittarius

341. His favorite rendition of *The Star Spangled Banner* is by?

    a. Robert Merrill
    b. Celine Dion
    c. Frank Sinatra

342. What was the license plate on Jack's new Mercedes convertible?

    a. TRADERJACK1
    b. CHAMPS03
    c. MARLINS15

Answers
337a 338b 339c 340c 341a 342b

343. His favorite holiday movie is?

    a. White Christmas
    b. Miracle On 34th Street
    c. The Bells of St. Mary's

344. Jack's wife received a certificate from the Mayor of Elon, recognizing her as?

    a. baseball's number one wife
    b. the first lady of major league baseball
    c. Mrs. Major League Baseball

345. What did Jack give to President Bush when the team visited the White House in January 2004?

    a. a Marlins team jacket
    b. a cigar
    c. a Marlins shirt with number 1 on it

Answers
343b 344b 345b

Jack Is Honored In Different Halls of Fame

He is a member of four Hall of Fames: St. Mary's High School Hall of Fame, New Jersey Sportswriters Hall of Fame, North Carolina Sports Hall of Fame, and the Sports Hall of Fame of New Jersey.

Did You Know?

Jack was the first person in the history of Elon, North Carolina to receive a key to the town. He also received keys to Miami and Fort Lauderdale.

Whistle Blower

Jack was a basketball official back in the 1950's and 1960's during the off-season. He even refereed some Atlantic Coast Conference games.

February 2000-Jack is shown delivering his acceptance speech to the New Jersey Sportswriters Association after being chosen by them as "Manager of The Year." He also received the Distinguished Service to Baseball Award.

What Jack McKeon-Managed Team Did They Play For ?
Part 1

Fill in the blank with: c-Cincinnati; f-Florida; k-Kansas City; o-Oakland; s-San Diego.

346. ___ Rob Bell

347. ___ Tim Spooneybarger

348. ___ Harmon Killebrew

349. ___ Doc Medich

350. ___ Tito Fuentes

351. ___ John Kruk

Answers
346c 347f 348k 349o 350o 351s

352. ___ Nate Bump

353. ___ Ron Villone

354. ___ Mark Redman

355. ___ Mark Portugal

356. ___ Mike Pagliarulo

357. ___ Todd Hollandsworth

358. ___ Buck Martinez

359. ___ Lindy McDaniel

360. ___ Willie Crawford

361. ___ Tony Solaita

What Jack McKeon-Managed Team Did They Play For? Part 2

Fill in the blanks with C-Cincinnati; F-Florida; K-Kansas City; O-Oakland; S-San Diego.

362. ___ Stan Bahnsen

363. ___ Gary Martz

364. ___ Miguel Dilone

365. ___ Juan Encarnacion

366. ___ Ray Sadecki

367. ___ Chris Stynes

Answers
352f 353c 354f 355c 356s 357f 358k 359k
360o 361k 362o 363k 364o 365f 366k 367c

368. ___ Dickie Thon

369. ___ Braden Looper

370. ___ Eddie Taubensee

371. ___ Jamie Quirk

372. ___ Mark Parent

373. ___ Willie Horton

374. ___ Pokey Reese

375. ___ Mitchell Page

376. ___ Rich McKinney

377. ___ Elmer Dessens

378. ___ Orlando Cepeda

What Jack McKeon-Managed Team Did They Play For Part 3

Fill in the blanks with C-Cincinnati; F-Florida; K-Kansas City; O-Oakland; S-San Diego

379. ___ Denny Neagle

380. ___ Keith Moreland

381. ___ Nelson Briles

382. ___ Alex Ochoa

383. ___ Mike Jorgenson

Answers

368s 369f 370c 371k 372s 373o 374c 375o
376o 377c 378k 379c 380s 381k 382c 383o

384.___Pete Harnisch

385.___Dock Ellis

386.___Hal Morris

387.___Ivan Rodriguez

388.___Scott Sullivan

389.___Randy Ready

390.___Mike Morgan

391.___Scott Williamson

392.___Rich Scheinblum

393.___Vida Blue

394.___Andy Fox

395.___Derrek Lee

What Jack McKeon-Managed Team Did They Play For? Part 4

Fill in the blanks with C-Cincinnati; F-Florida; K-Kansas City; O-Oakland; S-San Diego.

396.___Earl Williams

397.___Dennis Leonard

398.___Mike Torrez

399.___Shawn Abner

Answers
384c 385o 386c 387f 388c 389s 390o 391c
392k 393o 394f 395f 396o 397k 398o 399s

400.___Brian Johnson

401.___Don Schulze

402.___Frank White

403.___Calvin Schiraldi

404.___Rick Reichardt

405.___Andy Benes

406.___Stan Jefferson

407.___Derek Lilliquist

408.___Chris Brown

409.___George Throop

410.___Marvel Wynne

What Jack McKeon-Managed Team Did They Play For? Part 5

Fill in the blanks with C-Cincinnati; F-Florida; K-Kansas City; O-Oakland; S-San Diego.

411.___Joey Cora

412.___Dante Bichette

413.___Dick Allen

414.___Lance McCullers

415.___Abraham Nunez

Answers

400c 401s 402k 403s 404k 405s 406s 407s
408s 409k 410s 411s 412c 413o 414s 415f

416.___Justin Wayne

417.___Damon Easley

418.___Wil Cordero

Do You Know The Florida Marlins 2003 Team Leaders?

Match the hitting leaders and categories which they led the team in 2003. Fill in the blanks, using: c-Luis Castillo; e-Juan Encarnacion; l-Mike Lowell; p-Juan Pierre.

419.___Batting Average

420.___Slugging Percentage

421.___Runs

422.___Hits

423.___RBI

424.___Home Runs

425.___Doubles

426.___Triples

427.___Stolen Bases

Match the following 2003 pitching leaders using: b-Josh Beckett; l-Braden Looper; pa-Carl Pavano; pe-Brad Penny; r-Mark Redman; u-Ugueth Urbina; w-Dontrelle Willis.

428.___Innings Pitched

429.___Wins

430.___Saves

431.___ ERA

432.___ Strikeouts

1962: McKeon's Radio Made Baseball History

On July 18, 1962, Jack McKeon, innovative baseball manager of the Vancouver Mounties in the Pacific Coast League, made baseball history. McKeon conceived the idea of dugout to diamond communication, which was using an audio device to give his pitcher pitch-by-pitch instructions during the second game of a doubleheader against the Tacoma Giants.

At the time, the experiment was legal. No baseball law mentioned the use of radio aids, and McKeon's transmitter was licensed (XM11495) by the Department of Transport. Ford Frick, who at the time was Commissioner of Baseball, when asked to comment said he would defer his opinion of the device until he knew more about it.

Introduction of the radio unit came before a crowd of 3,188 fans, none of whom even suspected what was taking place. Players and umpires were also unaware of the baseball history being made. The secret was so closely guarded that even the Mountie players learned that their team was taking organized baseball into a new frontier, only seconds before the second game.

McKeon was invited to appear on the "I've Got A Secret," and "What's My Line" TV shows in September. A feature article on his baseball innovation appeared in *The Sporting News*, *Time* and *Life* magazines.

Looking Back At McKeon's First Major League Club: The 1973 Kansas City Royals

It took Jack McKeon 19 years of long bus rides in the minor leagues, but he finally achieved his dream of managing in the major leagues in 1973 with the Kansas City Royals. Owner Ewing Kauffman was very impressed with Jack's credentials and decided to give him a shot at the big time.

McKeon did not disappoint. He guided the Royals to an excellent 88-74, record to take second place in the AL West, finishing only six games behind the Oakland Athletics.

The Players

The starters were: Fran Healy-catcher; John Mayberry-first base; Cookie Rojas-second base; Freddie Patek-shortstop; Paul Schaal-third base; Ed Kirkpatrick-left field; Amos Otis-center field; Lou Piniella-right field; The

DH's were Hal McRae and Gail Hopkins. The top starting pitchers were: Paul Splittorff, Steve Busby, and Dick Drago. The closers were Doug Bird and Gene Garber.

Reserve players throughout the season were: Steve Hovley, Kurt Bevacqua, Carl Taylor, Frank White, Bobby Floyd, Jim Wohlford, Rick Reichardt, Tom Poquette, Buck Martinez, rookie George Brett, Jerry May, Frank Ortenzio, Keith Marshall.

Other pitchers who saw action in '73 were: Al Fitzmorris, Ken Wright, Wayne Simpson, Bruce Dal Canton, Steve Mingori, Joe Hoerner, Mark Littell, Mike Jackson, Norm Angelini, Tom Burgmeier, Barry Raziano. McKeon's coaching staff consisted of Harry Dunlop, Charlie Lau, and Galen Cisco, the pitching coach.

"Trader Jack's" Padres Win First National League Pennant

1984-The San Diego Padres, through the brilliant acquisitions and free agent signings of GM "Trader Jack" McKeon, won the first pennant in franchise history, defeating the tough Chicago Cubs. San Diego won the West Division title with a 92-70 mark under manager Dick Williams. Trailing two games to none in the best of five NLCS, they battled back to win the next three games, and take the NL title.

The powerful Detroit Tigers spoiled San Diego's tremendous run, by beating them four games to one in the World Series.

The Players

The starting players were: Terry Kennedy-catcher; Steve Garvey-first base; Alan Wiggins-second base; Garry Templeton-shortstop; Graig Nettles-third base; Tony Gwynn, Kevin McReynolds, and Carmelo Martinez-outfielders.

The starting pitchers with the most victories were: Eric Show, Mark Thurmond, Ed Whitson, Tim Lollar, and Andy Hawkins. The top save specialists were Goose Gossage, Craig Lefferts, and Dave Dravecky.

Other position players who performed during the season were: Luis Salazar, Tim Flannery, Bobby Brown, Kurt Bevacqua, Mario Ramirez, Champ Summers, Bruce Bochy, Eddie Miller, Ron Roenicke, Doug Gwosdz.

Pitchers who also saw action throughout the year were: Dave Dravecky, Greg Harris, Sid Monge, Luis DeLeon, Floyd Chiffer, Greg Booker.

Jack had his own weekly radio show when he was with the San Diego Padres in the 1980's, called "The Trader Jack Show." Pictured is Jack (l) and Jim Williams from Toyota.

Jack McKeon Celebrates 50 Years In Pro Baseball
An Exclusive Interview
By Tom Burkard

(Article appeared in the June, 1999 issue of *The South Amboy-Sayreville Times*)

On Memorial Day, May 31st, I had the honor and most pleasant experience of meeting Cincinnati Reds manager and South Amboy native, Jack McKeon for the first time. The interview took place in the manager's office of the Reds' clubhouse at Shea Stadium, my first time ever in that big league environment. It proved most interesting and insightful on McKeon's 50 star-studded years of professional baseball excellence. It was a day I will never forget, and although we had not met before, Jack made me feel comfortable, and when I left, I felt like we had been friends for years.

TB: Born and raised in South Amboy, New Jersey, I'm sure our readers would like to know if have special memories of those good old days that may stand out?

JM: I talk about South Amboy all the time. This is where we got our start. It's a tribute to the people of South Amboy and to the city administrators for giving us opportunities to have facilities and encouraging us with city leagues they offered. It enabled us to pursue our dream. I remember growing up there and my father starting McKeon Boys Club during the War to keep us off the streets. He got the city council to give us fields and gyms on certain days. We had 15 or 16 kids. You see the O'Brien Twins, myself, my brother went to AAA ball. Leo Kedzierski, Ray Stockton. Out of that team, eight went into pro baseball, three into the big leagues.

TB: Now in your 50th year of pro baseball, how has the game changed since you broke in back in 1949?

JM: All the guys are bigger and stronger today. The love of the game is not as great as it used to be when we broke in. Now it's money. I don't think the guys eat, sleep and drink baseball like we did. Now it's a money situation, where everybody wants to make all the money. The unselfishness is not there like it used to be. The camaraderie amongst players is not what it used to be, because now they're all millionaires and go their own separate ways. We used to hang around all the time together.

TB: St. Mary's High School has produced five big leaguers, and Sayreville of course, sent Ed "Buddy" Popowski to the Red Sox. Do you ever run into Allie Clark, The O'Brien Twins, Tom Kelly or Popowski?

JM: I haven't seen "Buddy" recently, but Allie came down to Florida last year, and I visited with him. I ran into the O'Briens in Seattle a few years ago, and saw Eddie last year in Chicago. Kelly, I see all the time. In fact, we're going to play the Twins in Minnesota next week.

TB: Kelly and yourself spent plenty of time in the minors, playing, coaching and managing. He got a cup of coffee with the Twins in '74 for about a month. Why would you say that many fine managers, like yourself, Kelly, Walter Alston, Leyland and LaSorda have done so well despite little or no big league playing experience?

JM: I think we all analyzed our abilities and realized that the dream of playing in the big leagues was going to be remote, and how do you get there? In my case, when I realized I wasn't going to make it as a player, I kept my goal the same, but changed direction. I decided that I wanted to go to the big leagues as a manager. I think we studied the game, weren't great players, but had the ability to observe, knowing that, hey, we're not going to be the star players. But we had the chance to make it in a different way. I just won my 600th game about two weeks ago, and they gave me a plaque in Cincinnati.

TB: What was it like managing for owners like Charlie Finley, The Krocs, and Marge Schott?

JM: There is no one like Charlie Finley. He was a very eccentric owner, a hands on type guy, and liked to control you day and night. A good guy, he made you a better manager because you had to stay on your toes. He constantly second guessed you, whether you were right or wrong. With Charlie, you were always wrong, even if you were right. We had a good relationship.

Kroc was a great person. I took over in San Diego as GM in '80, and the first thing Ray Kroc said to me was, 'I don't know anything about this game. Do what you think is right, don't ask me.' He gave me carte blanche. I took the ball and ran with it. I'm sorry he died before we won our first pennant in '84. It was his dream to get to the World Series.

TB: Your '99 Reds seem like they're loaded with young talent. How far can they go?

JM: Over the last two years, we developed a number of good, young players, like the Caseys, Reeses, Williamsons, and Reyes,' so we're on the right track. We went out and got Vaughn and Nagle this year. We've got to continue to put young kids in the lineup, and struggle with them for awhile, but the fruits of our labor will payoff down the road. How good can we be? Who knows? If our pitching comes through, which is the name of the game, we've got a chance to maybe compete for the Wild Card, but it's a long shot.

TB: So far this year, your first baseman, Sean Casey has been near the top in the NL in batting average, and several other categories. How good is he, and will he even get better?

JM: The guy's incredible! He's tremendous! My son Kasey was scouting for the Indians, and signed him. He's a fine hitter, probably the best young hitter I've ever managed except for Tony Gwynn. This guy has incredible eyesight, great knowledge of the strike zone, and makes adjustments at the plate himself. He's very focused and is very sharp, personality wise, outstanding! He's an All-American boy. He smiles, loves to play the game, and is always having fun, that's why I think he's a success.

TB: One of your sons played pro ball. How far did he go?

JM: Kasey played three or four years. He signed with the Tigers, played a few years with them, went over and played a year or two with Seattle. He then managed at Reno in the California League, and had an opportunity to take a scouting job, and that's what he likes to do, so he's been scouting for a number of years. He's only about 31 years old.

TB: Outside of being the Padres GM in '84 when they won the NL crown, what's been your biggest thrill in baseball?

JM: Managing the '88 Padres. When I took them over in New York on May 26th, they were 18 games under .500, and ended up five over .500. It was a great comeback!

TB: What is the best team you ever managed in the big leagues?

JM: My first year with Kansas City was an exciting year. We finished second place with 88 wins, the most they ever had at that time.

TB: Should Pete Rose be in the Hall of Fame?

JM: I think he should be in the Hall of Fame on athletic ability. His off-field activities sometimes hurt him a little bit, but what he did on-field, certainly warrants he be in there.

TB: Do you have any future goals for yourself and the Reds?

JM: Certainly I'd like to stay around long enough to see them win. I play it one year at a time. I enjoy the hell out of working with the young guys. That's a big key. I'll stay as long as they want me, and it's fun.

TB: In your 50 years of baseball, have you ever managed any Hall-of-Famers?

JM: Every year. I had Killebrew, Carew, Brett and Tony Gwynn, who will eventually make it. Some other guys who got close are Kaat and Oliva, but they never made it. I was hoping Gwynn would get his 3,000th hit when we were out there. He's a great guy!

TB: How did they start calling you Mc-Key-on instead of the way our locals call you Mc-Qu-en?

JM: When "Biff" (Jack's Brother) and I are sometimes at the same banquet, I get a kick out of them introducing him as Bill Mc-Q-en, and they introduce me as Jack Mc-Key-on, then say we're brothers. When I first left South Amboy and played minor league ball in Alabama, they called me Mc-Key-on, and when I went to Carolina, they called me Mc-Key-on.

TB: After all is said and done, how would you like Jack McKeon to be remembered?

JM: I'd like to be remembered as a guy who really appreciated his roots in South Amboy. God bless the people there that gave me encouragement and the opportunity to play. When I'm talking to kids, I tell them if you have a dream, you can reach it if you work at it, and dedicate yourself to hard work.

TB: What gave you the motivation to succeed and make it to the major leagues?

JM: When I signed in '49 and went away to play ball, and would come home to visit during the season, I would run into Joey Crowe and some old guys, and people in town, and they'd always tell me how they were following me through my father, and how proud of me my parents were, that I was having success. That was the impetus that kept me going. They said it couldn't be done, and I proved them wrong. I constantly had my goal to bust my tail to make it, and make my parents proud.

*Editors Note: And make it he did! All of South Amboy is proud of Jack McKeon for his great accomplishments, and for always remembering his roots in town. Jack McKeon is one truly class act, to whom we always wish continued success and happiness!

Talkin' Baseball With Jack McKeon
An SA Times Special Interview
By Tom Burkard

(Article appeared in the September 18, 1999 issue of *The South Amboy-Sayreville Times*)

While on our trip to see the Philadelphia Phillies and Cincinnati Reds baseball game on September 4th, we never dreamt that we would be witnessing baseball history in the making, that evening at Veterans Stadium.

The interview, only my second meeting with South Amboy native and perhaps baseball's best manager, Jack McKeon, was upbeat, enlightening and fun, with the cigar-smoking skipper, as we chatted in the Reds dugout, with rain falling, three hours before game time. As you will see, I questioned him about several interesting subjects including home runs and the lively ball, but neither of us could have predicted the record-breaking performance that would follow on that memorable evening.

Who was to know that McKeon's Reds would go on a home run rampage, and shatter the National League record that evening, as well as setting a couple of other marks over the weekend?

TB: How does it feel to be in the pennant race once again?

JM: No question about it, it feels great! September is the time you always look forward to. It's something to shoot for. Most of the time in September, you're dragging your feet and trying to play the string out. Now we're playing everyday.

TB: The so-called baseball experts did not expect the '99 Reds to be much of a challenger for the NL West title. Why has your club excelled and proven critics wrong?

JM: We have a lot of young guys that have made tremendous progress. Some guys are having career years. Probably the biggest reason is the development of our younger players.

TB: Besides Tony Gwynn and your own players, who do you feel are the top three players in the bigs?

JM: There's so many good ones! You've got different types of players like the Bagwells, the Piazzas, Venturas, Griffeys, Matt Williamses. There's an awful lot of good players, and you can't single one out.

TB: Did you ever expect McGwire and Sosa to hit so many homers again this year?

JM: Well, they're big, strong guys with tremendous power. They programmed themselves to be home run hitters. When you look around baseball, McGwire and Sosa, and maybe Griffey and Piazza have that kind of power. There's only a handful of guys that you can say will hit 50 or more homers.

TB: Why are there so many homers today, as compared to years ago? Is the ball juiced up?

JM: I think the ball is juiced, and some of the new parks are smaller. Also, pitching has been diluted because of expansion. The players are bigger and stronger than they were before.

TB: What team do you hope to face in the first round of the playoffs?

JM: We just got to make it. We don't care who we're going to play. (Jokingly) The House of David if we have to!

TB: What was your highlight so far of this great '99 season?

JM: I'm real proud of the fact that two of our young players made the All Star team. Sean Casey and Scott Williamson. It kind of set the pace for the kind of year we had.

TB: How do you think the new umpires will affect play through the end of the season?

JM: I don't think that there'll be that much of a difference, really. There might be a few more gripes and complaints on balls and strikes for their inexperience, but I don't see that much difference.

TB: Always a creative mind and innovator, what would you suggest to improve the game?

JM: Do away with the DH. Go back to the 154-game season. Also cut the player limit to 23.

TB: What major league records do you feel will never be broken?

JM: I don't think Ripken's record will be broken. We don't have those kind of players today that want to go out there everyday. 500 wins will be tough. Randy Johnson will come closest to Ryan's strikeout mark, if he stays healthy and is around long enough.

Jack McKeon (r) talks baseball with two of his best friends, the late Ed "Buddy" Popowski (l) and Allie Clark (c) at a Card Show/Fundraiser for the South Amboy First Aid on February 5, 2000, at Christ Church Hall. Popowski was a manager, coach, special instructor and much more for 65 years with the Boston Red Sox organization. Allie won two World Series rings in 1947 with the Yankees, and in '48 with Cleveland. On this day, the three ballplayers signed autographs for four hours to help the First Aid.

McKeon's Reds Set New NL Records At Philly
By Tom Burkard

(Article appeared in the September 18, 1999 issue of *The South Amboy-Sayreville Times*)

South Amboy's native son, Jack McKeon, who happens to be the baseball manager of the highly talented Cincinnati Reds major league baseball club, recently had a most memorable trip to the Philadelphia Phillies Veterans Stadium.

On Saturday night, September 4th, McKeon's fired-up contingent of super-fine ballplayers, unleashed a mammoth power display by blasting a new National League record of nine home runs into the Philly air, as Cincinnati romped to a 22-3 triumph over the Phils.

Catcher, Ed Taubensee paved the way with two dingers, while Greg Vaughn, Jersey product, Jeffrey Hammonds, Aaron Boone, Dmitri Young, Pokey Reese, Brian Johnson and Mark Lewis all cranked one homer apiece in the "Dinger Derby of '99.

The Reds also set records with the 22 runs (the most runs scored by an opponent at Veterans Stadium), and the nine homers were also the most by a Philadelphia opponent.

After the game, McKeon, who is celebrating his 50th year in professional baseball this season, visited near the third base seats with the large entourage of family, friends and fans who trekked to Philly. "Congratulations!" "Nice game!" "Great going!" "Way to go," could be heard all over from Jack's faithful followers, many from the South Amboy/Sayreville area. The jubilant skipper said that, "It was nice," and he'd never seen so many homers in a game.

The Reds home run surge continued on Sunday, September 5th, as they crunched five more round-trippers to set a major league mark for two games with an impressive 14 HR's. Hammonds hammered two, Vaughn, Young, and Taubensee all homered for the second consecutive day to be part of yet another record-breaking performance. Cincinnati topped the previous mark, which was held jointly by the 1939 Yankees and the 1961 San Francisco Giants.

McKeon Wins Manager Of The Year Awards
By Tom Burkard

(Article appeared in the November 1999 issue of *The South Amboy-Sayreville Times*)

South Amboy's native son, Jack McKeon recently won the prestigious BBWAA 1999 National League Manager of the Year Award, and also the Associated Press' 1999 Manager of the Year Award.

Jack watches intently as his hitters prep for an upcoming game.
(Photo courtesy of Cincinnati Reds)

A 1948 graduate of St. Mary's High School, where he was an All-County, All-State catcher, McKeon did an incredible job this season, his 50th year in pro baseball. He guided the Cincinnati Reds to 96 victories, and took them to within one game of a playoff spot, before bowing to the New York Mets, in a Wild Card tie-breaker.

Jack said, "It's real nice to receive this kind of award. A lot of it goes to the players. You're only as good as your players, and we had good players."

Cincinnati's 96 wins was the most for the Reds since the Big Red Machine in 1976, and definitely proved McKeon's managerial brilliance, as the club was not picked to fare too well in 1999 pre-season polls.

Jack received a one-year contract extension from Cincinnati recently.

Plans are currently in the early stages, but a sports memorabilia show, featuring Jack in person, signing autographs, an auction, and also a dinner in his honor will be held at a location to be announced. All proceeds will go to the First Aid Squad.

McKeon definitely loves his hometown of South Amboy, and is donating his time to come to these events and help the South Amboy First Aid raise money.

The local communities should be very proud of Jack and his tremendous achievements, and hopefully come out and meet this wonderful celebrity at "Jack McKeon Day," on February 5, 2000, and also help the First Aid.

New Jersey Sportswriters' Hall of Fame Induction Speech

On February 6, 2000, Jack McKeon was inducted into the New Jersey Sportswriters Association's Hall of Fame at a dinner attended by over 1,000 at The Pines in Edison, New Jersey. He also received the National League Manager of the Year award from the Association. Jack's outstanding speech follows:

"We had a tremendous group last year that did a marvelous job. Outstanding coaches, outstanding players, great camaraderie. We won 96 games and had to run into Al Leiter in the 97th game and got eked out. It was a great run, a great time, and we're looking forward to going again.

I think the guy that had the most influence on the O'Brien Twins and myself when we were youngsters in grade school was Allie Clark. We watched him play in high school, and as he started up the professional ladder, we all wanted to emulate him. As he succeeded to the major leagues, it was just the push we needed. We realized that this was something great. This guy from our town was doing such a great job, we wanted to be like him. Maybe, even though he doesn't realize it, he had a tremendous influence on our lives and is probably the reason we got to the big leagues. Thanks, Allie!

I signed in '49 and played a few years. I had a tough time with the bat. Some years, I didn't hit my weight. A couple of years I hit .300- .150 right-handed, and .150 left-handed. I ran into Danny Murtaugh when I was in Spring Training in 1953 at New Orleans. I think Danny might have saw a future for me. I kind of analyzed myself. I think the best job I ever did was scouting myself. I realized then I wasn't about to make the major leagues as a player, so I kept my goal the same, but changed my direction, and decided I was going to go through the manager's field. Danny Murtaugh said one day, 'Hey you ever think about managing?' And I said, 'Yeah, the way I hit, I guess I ought to.' He said, 'Well, I'll recommend you to Mr. Rickey.'

The following year, I ended up getting my job. I started managing at 24 years old after playing only 4 1/2 seasons, and I'm still at it. I did take a siesta for a few years. I took a 9-year break before I came back to San Diego, and a 7-year break before I came back to here (to Cincinnati). What I realized during the breaks is that I think we all mature after awhile. You get in a situation, day-in, and day-out, and all of a sudden, you get away from it for a few years. You mature a little bit. I think I did. I think I give more responsibility to my coaches now. I let coaches coach and players play. Plus the fact, I don't let little things bother me anymore. Maybe when I was an up and coming manager, starting my career in the big leagues, I was trying to impress people on how smart I was.

How good I was. I tried to impress on the players on how tough I could be, and kind of let little things get carried away. Now, I don't need the job. I enjoy what I'm doing. I have a lot of fun. Now, when I take a guy out of the game, and he gives me some crap, I have to turn away. I don't hear it. I don't see it. It don't bother me. Before I would challenge somebody. So, I think the big difference is we have matured in those areas. One of the greatest experiences I ever had in my life was managing for Charlie Finley. I think that every young minor league manager ought to spend one-year working for Charlie Finley, and I think they'd be well prepared for a long major league career. You could not win with Charlie. If you were right, you were wrong. It didn't make any difference. Every morning at 6 o'clock, you'd get the call. You gotta remember, he lived in Chicago and I was managing the Oakland A's, and every morning at 6 o'clock, you'd get the call. If you thought you did a heck of a job managing last night to win the game, it wasn't good enough, you did something wrong. It got to the point where I had Option A, Option B, Option C, Option D, Option E, because I knew damn well I was wrong on all those options, but at least, I could throw them at him.

Charlie focused on speed and brought in Herb Washington as DR (Designated Runner). He was probably the guy in modern day baseball that put the emphasis on speed. When I was managing in '77, we left Spring Training with our club, and normally, I 'd have a right-handed hitter, or left-handed hitter off the bench, or some extra reserves. I left with five "rabbits", as Charlie used to call anybody that could run, and anybody that couldn't was a "truck."

My orders from him was anytime late in a ballgame, and we had a guy who couldn't run, a "truck," get the "truck" off the field and put the "rabbit" in, and that's what I'd do. Anyway, we're playing in Minnesota and he called me over and said, 'I'm bringing a kid from Jersey City named Darrell Woodard. He stole 62 bases at Jersey City and is leading the International League.' He said 'I want you to run him every day with Dilone,' (my other runner). So, he said 'If you have to use this guy, only use him at second base, and he's not a good infielder and not good at second base, but don't play him at another place but second base.' A month later, we were playing in Oakland and it was the 8th inning, and we're ahead 3-2 against the Cleveland Indians. Our leadoff hitter, Wayne Gross singles. Well, he's a "truck." I had to get the "truck" out and put the "rabbit" in. Now the "rabbit's" gotta play because I've got no more infielders. So, he gets thrown out stealing and now we start the top of the 9th. Following Charlie's advice, I took my little second baseman, Mike Edwards off second, and moved him to third, and put the "rabbit" on second base. They got two men on and one out, and Johnny Grubb, a left-handed hitter comes up to pinch hit. So, I bring in Bob Lacey, a lefty pitcher, and put my regular double play combo together in hopes we'll get out of the inning, so I did it. The first pitch Lacey threw to Grubb, he hits a line drive to third base. Woodard jumped up, caught the ball, threw to second, the game's over-we won! Six o'clock the next morning, the telephone rings, 'McKeon, Finley. They're all laughing at you. The players are laughing at you, the media's laughing at you, everybody's laughing at you.' I said, what the hell are they laughing at, Charlie? He said, 'I told you not to play him at third base, I'm trying to help you become a good manager, but you went ahead and did it.' I said I only played him at third base for one pitch, and he said, 'how's that? He sees the paper in Chicago the next morning and sees the guy played third base. I explained, and then he paused for 15 seconds and said, 'I suppose you think you're a damn genius now.'

That's what you had to put up with everyday with Charlie Finley. It was a lot of fun, starting my 51st year this year. I've enjoyed every bit of it. I've had a lot of fun, and I'm still having fun. I've been blessed with a great wife and four young children, and a great group of supporters from South Amboy. I hope to stay in this game, continue to have fun, and work for you senior citizens."

2000 Sarasota, Florida-Superstar Ken Griffey Jr. (l), who was expected to lead the Reds to the World Series, takes a break from BP with manager McKeon.

Exclusive: Jack McKeon's Final Interview As Manager Of The Reds

By Tom Burkard

(Article appeared in the October 14, 2000 issue of *The South Amboy-Sayreville Times*)

I had the pleasure of visiting my good friend in Cincinnati, Jack McKeon, from September 21-24, and on September 23rd, nine days before the Reds fired him, he granted me an exclusive interview at the Regal Cincinnati Hotel lobby.

Jack knew that he would not be coming back in 2001 as manager of the Cincinnati Reds, and talked openly about it in the following interview:

TB: How does it feel to be going into the St. Mary's High School Athletic Hall of Fame?

JM: It's a great honor to go in with so many other great guys. Seeing Allie Clark in the majors spurred a lot of us, the O'Briens, myself, my brother Bill. Allie was a catalyst for all of us. It's nice to go in with a young fellow, Tom Kelly. He's had so much success at Minnesota, and the O'Briens, what they've done. It's something special to go in with this group. I'm honored to be in with all of them.

TB: Do you have anything planned for the off-season?

JM: My youngest son, Kasey is getting married November 4th. I'm going to take it easy. I'm going to Switzerland to visit my other son and his family. They've been there for two years, and it will be nice to see them. Basically, give up managing, enjoy life, and watch my grandkids grow up.

I'm not going to retire. I'll do something in baseball, but I'm going to get out of managing. I've had my share, and its been a lot of fun. There are other things in life you got to do.

TB: It was a pretty good year for the Reds considering. What went wrong?

JM: Lots of injuries, and the expectations were high with Griffey coming in, and we were supposed to automatically win and go to the World Series because we got Griffey. It doesn't work that way. We played only 14 games all season with our projected lineup we put together in Spring Training. All my key players were out with injuries throughout the year. It's tough to compete in our league if you're not healthy. Last year was spectacular because we were injury free. We couldn't get anything going, or generate any consistency.

TB: Will you miss the game?

JM: No. This is the third time I've backed out of managing. One time I laid back for seven years and another time for nine years. I'll miss the camaraderie you have, the writers. I'll travel around and enjoy a little bit. Maybe I'll get back to South Amboy more often, and stop at Atlantic City along the way.

Note: Jack McKeon was the 1999 National League Manager of the Year. His 2000 Cincy club was riddled by injuries, and turmoil caused by a couple of spoiled superstars. The fans loved and supported him as can be attested by the banners I saw hung around Cinergy Field, which said, "Bring Jack Back," and "We love Jack McKeon."

Through it all, the veteran skipper guided the Reds to 85 victories and a 2nd place finish in the NL Central Division, not bad by any standards, except top brass thought he should have done more, and fired him.

Jack has had an outstanding 51 years in pro baseball, and his accomplishments are more than most could dream. A truly dedicated, sincere and wonderful person, I wish Jack the best in whatever he does in the future, and have no doubt that he will continue to be a huge success. Congratulations on a tremendous career, Jack!

McKeon, Reds Part Ways

On October 2, 2000, Jack McKeon was let go by the Cincinnati Reds after leading the team to a 85-77 record and second place finish for the second consecutive year in the National League Central Division. McKeon was selected National League Manager of the Year in 1999 after leading the club to 96 victories.

Heavily-favored, Ken Griffey Sr. or third base coach, Ron Oester were projected to get the job, but Bob Boone was hired as McKeon's replacement.

Top-notch basketball broadcaster, Dick Vitale (r) visits his good friend, Jack McKeon during Spring Training 2000 in Sarasota, Florida.

Jack McKeon stands by the baseball field which was renamed in his honor on October 28, 2000. He spent many hours as a youngster honing his baseball skills on this field in South Amboy, New Jersey.

Veterans, McKeon Honored With Renaming of Field

(The following article appeared in the November 11, 2000 issue of *The South Amboy-Sayreville Times*)

On Saturday afternoon, October 28th, before a crowd of over 100 people, South Amboy Mayor John T. O'Leary in conjunction with local veterans organizations honored veterans, and Jack McKeon, a United States Air Force veteran, by renaming Vets Field to Veterans Memorial Park, Home of Jack McKeon Field.

O'Leary said, "We are honoring the men and women who gave the supreme sacrifice for their country. We will honor them on a far greater scope by changing it to a memorial park. We will also honor Jack McKeon, a distinguished Air Force veteran, who rose to the rank of Sergeant, and in 1951, guided Sampson Air Force Base, New York to the Air Force World Series championship. He has been in pro baseball for 51 years, is an outstanding role model for the youth, and in February of this year returned to South Amboy, and helped raise over $7,000 for the First Aid with other local big leaguers, Allie Clark and Ed "Buddy" Popowski."

The color guards from the Luke A. Lovely American Legion Post #62 of South Amboy, and South Amboy Disabled American Veterans presented a 21-gun salute for the sailors who recently lost their lives on the USS Cole.

Mayor O'Leary presented proclamations to the City's Veterans Alliance and McKeon, and stated, "this event gave people the opportunity to reflect on the sacrifices veterans have made to preserve democracy."

McKeon thanked South Amboy's past and present administration, the veterans, and Allie Clark who "is the guy who gave us something to shoot at. We were high school kids and he was a major leaguer. He was our idol, and inspired us to work at it," said McKeon.

McKeon most recently managed the Cincinnati Reds, and was the 1999 National League "Manager of The Year. His major league won-lost record is a respectable 770-733.

St. Mary's High School Athletic Hall of Fame Induction

Jack McKeon was inducted into St. Mary's High School's Athletic Hall of Fame at its inaugural ceremony on October 28, 2000. The following is Jack's speech in its entirety:

"Well, it's nice to be here, back again. It's nice to see so many of my friends out here. Most of these guys and gals have taken a lot of my stories. Allie Clark is up here talking about some gal chasing him. I have a girl in North Carolina, that's why I'm stuck down there. When I played down there, she chased me and we're celebrating our 46th Wedding Anniversary tomorrow.

I'd like to thank my family and friends, brother and sister, brothers-in-law, cousins and what have you. Thank you for showing up. Also, I'd like to thank the committee for putting me among these fine people up here in the Hall of Fame. It's certainly an honor. But, I think a lot of the credit belongs to you people out there, really. I've seen so many friends tonight, guys and gals that I went to school with and graduated with. And seeing so many of our former supporters, people that supported us when we were youngsters here in this area.

South Amboy's had a great tradition, and St. Mary's also had a great tradition, as far as athletics go. We're extremely proud that five of us are involved in baseball, and mainly that we speak on the baseball side, because we had a lot going for us in our day. We had a lot of professional baseball players in this area, guys like Joey Crowe, Pete Pavich, The Rogers brothers, the Zebro brothers and this guy sitting here, Allie Clark. They gave us a lot of motivation. We'd see stories written about these guys and they kind of gave us that motivating force to imitate these guys.

When Allie got to the big leagues, here we were, as Allie said, 'we were playing right here in this field, right under us here, (the old St. Mary's baseball field was located right beneath where the gym is currently located). We were working hard and dedicating ourselves, because we saw what he was providing for us. That dream, and because of his efforts, we were fortunate enough to work our way up and do the same thing that he did. So, it's all as Tom Kelly said, 'It's friendships, it's cooperation,' and if it wasn't for the mayor and council, the recreation's backing, to provide us the fields, basketball courts to play on, and keep us out of trouble.

There is also a certain dedication, and I can speak because we're sitting up here, the two O'Briens and myself. You know its very rare as Allie said, to get five people that have played in the major leagues out of one school. Well, how about three out of one graduating class of about 65? I think it goes back to having that dream. You want to follow that dream. I can say that to these guys here, John and Eddie O'Brien, and myself, we were dedicated. We were out working from six in the morning till 12 o'clock at night, even as far as going to the circle in the Sayreville area by the Edison Bridge and playing baseball at night under the Parkway lights. Then someone mentioned about playing in a garage. Yeah, my father had a place on Leffert Street, it's still there. I went by the other day. A little building that used to house his trucks and snow plows and stuff. We'd get the key and move them all outside, and go in and take batting practice. Of course, the O'Briens got me in trouble because they put out a couple of windows, but we had a lot of fun.

I want to say hey, thanks to all of you for showing up tonight. These gentlemen and ladies up here who were recipients of being put into the Hall of Fame, we've had a lot of fun. It's great! As Tom Kelly said, 'It's getting back and renewing friendships, that's what it's all about.' Once again, we want to thank Allie and all those professional players that were before us for giving us and showing us the way. Thank you!"

On October 28, 2000, St. Mary's High School of South Amboy, NJ presented its Inaugural Athletic Hall of Fame Dinner/Induction Ceremony. The proud inductees included standing (l-r) Tom Kelly, Jack McKeon, George Krzyzanowski, Tom Scully, John O'Brien, Allie Clark, Ed O'Brien, Jack Kreiger. Seated (l-r) Eillen Fallon Seitz, Kathy Redling, Jean Ryan Zdanewicz (wife of the late John Zdanewicz), and Ellen Eppinger Eichele (daughter of the late Charley Eppinger).

Talkin' Baseball With Jack McKeon & Former Yankee Allie Clark

By Tom Burkard

(Article appeared in the August 2002 issue of *The South Amboy-Sayreville Times*)

What a thrill! I was honored to get a phone call from Marge Gorczyca, asking me if I would like to come over with Allie Clark, because her brother, Jack McKeon was coming up from North Carolina for a visit, and would like to see the both of us.

The last time I saw Jack was at his October 2000 incduction into St. Mary's Athletic Hall of Fame, and it was super to see him again! Allie was also happy to see the former big league baseball manager/GM.

The visit was most pleasant with plenty of great stories from South Amboy's major leaguers. Jack and Allie caught up on what's been going on in the world of baseball, and also about their mutual baseball friends, including Hall of Famer, Enos Slaughter, who recently passed away, Hank Bauer and several others. The tales of their days in professional ball were some of the most interesting I have ever heard.

McKeon mentioned that he coached Jim "Kitty" Kaat in 1959, his rookie year in the minors, and he knew that Jim would be a future major leaguer. Chuck Dressen and Joe Haines, a pitching guru came to watch Kaat pitch, and he won 3-0 on a 3-hitter, as Jack belted two homers. Afterwards, McKeon asked Haines what he thought about "Kitty," and he said, 'pretty good, but he'll never make it to the bigs." Jack bet Haines a steak dinner that Kaat would make the majors within two years, and McKeon's prediction came true only six months later, when Kaat was called to the Washington Senators. Jack proudly stated that, "He was there (in the majors) for 23 years, and won nearly 300 games, and 18 Golden Gloves."

McKeon and Clark talked about everything ranging from players' meal money, Allie got $8 a day when he played in the late 1940's and early 1950's, and Jack received a whopping $68 per diem in his last year with the Reds in 2000. They were in agreement on many baseball topics including random testing for steroids and drugs, and the possible strike, which they hope does not occur.

Will he ever get back into pro baseball? "When teams call me, I tell them to call me in six months and I'll see how I feel. The big thing today is who you work for. I'm not going to work for a bunch of wimps! Management has got to take control of the ballclub, and quit letting the inmates run the asylum," said McKeon.

When asked who would win the World Series this year, if there is one, Allie said, "The Yankees should win the AL, and Atlanta who will be tough in Series, should take the NL." McKeon picked a repeat of the Yankees-Arizona Diamondbacks in the World Series, with the Yankees winning this year.

It was easy to notice the tremendous respect these two gentlemen had for each other, as they rehashed memorable moments from their professional careers, and also the good old days in South Amboy.

When Jack McKeon was growing up in town, Allie Clark was his idol, and Jack never forgets to thank Allie when they meet. He said, "Allie, I want to thank you for being an inspiration to me and all the other kids when we were growing up. Seeing you playing pro ball with the Newark Bears and then with the Yankees gave us something to shoot for, something to believe in. You really gave us motivation to work hard like you did, and become professional athletes." Allie said, "It's always great to see you, Jack."

The talkin' baseball reunion with Jack McKeon and Allie Clark was a truly wonderful get-together that I will never forget.

McKeon's Thoughts On Possible Strike In 2002

(Excerpted from an August 2002 interview)

"I don't think they'll strike. I think the players realize there's too much at stake. They got things going in their favor. I hope they don't strike."

Jack Discusses The Possible Franchise Moves by Minnesota and Montreal In 2002

(Excerpted from an August 2002 interview)

"I really think northern Virginia is dying for a baseball team. There's some towns out there that would take Montreal and do much better. Why not move it to a city that wants it."

General Manager Or Manager?

When asked, 'What position did you prefer, general manager or manager?' Jack answered, "I liked both jobs, but managing better. I liked the daily challenge, the competitiveness. You'd come to the ballpark and it made you feel younger. You didn't have to sit in a chair and answer the telephone. This way you're out there, front and center of attention."

McKeon Praises Barry Bonds

(Excerpted from an August 2002 interview)

Jack McKeon respects and admires mega-superstar, Barry Bonds. While he was in between managerial jobs in 2002, he spoke very highly of the Giants' hero. "He's got such a quick bat. Everything about hitting- he waits, he's quick and he never swings at a bad pitch. People wanna say steroids and stuff, but I don't think that had anything to do with it. I think his natural talents have taken over."

Random Drug Testing? McKeon Says Yes!

(Excerpted from an August 2002 interview)

Jack McKeon is definitely in favor of having random drug testing in Major League Baseball. He said that, "They should have random testing for steroids and drugs too. You've got guys that are supposed to be role models, and if you're afraid to be tested, there's something wrong. I've said that all along. How can the union continue to support drug addicts, guys that have failed drug tests, and habitual drug users? How can they support them and fight for these guys? That's showing the country that these guys are model citizens."

McKeon Signs With Marlins
By Tom Burkard

(Article appeared in the May 24, 2003 issue of *The South Amboy-Sayreville Times*)

South Amboy native, Jack McKeon, signed to manage the Florida Marlins Major League Baseball Club, after being away from the game for two years.

McKeon last managed the Cincinnati Reds to a second place finish with a respectable 85-77 record in 2000. The Marlins are the fifth team that Jack has skippered. He was also the top gun at Kansas City, Oakland and San Diego, and has a career won-lost record of 770-733, .512, and ranks #64 on the All-Time list in wins, and #54 in winning percentage.

The 72-year old McKeon is the oldest manager in baseball, and the third oldest ever, behind Hall of Famers, Connie Mack and Casey Stengel. No one has taken a manager's job at such an advanced age. Those facts don't phase Jack at all. He said that being around the younger players makes him feel like he was 45 years old. "You're only as old as you feel. Age is just a number," he stated.

McKeon was a standout all-around athlete on St. Mary's legendary 1948 baseball and basketball teams, and was inducted into St. Mary's Athletic Hall of Fame at the Inaugural Banquet in 2000.

Jack was the National League Manager of the Year, and also the Associated Press' Manager of the Year in 1999, when he guided the Reds to 96 victories.

The Marlins had been struggling this year under ex-manager, Jeff Torborg, who is also a New Jersey native. McKeon will have his work cut out for him, as he tries to help Florida turn its season around. He stressed the fact that he's not a "miracle worker," and had a lot of work to do to get the club to "another level." If you consider his outstanding record and unsurpassed knowledge of the game, don't be surprised to see the Marlins' fortunes on the rise in the near future. Jack McKeon is a masterful evaluator of talent, and really knows how to handle the players. It's great to see our local hero back at the helm, where he belongs on a major league team.

He certainly has done some fine charitable works to help South Amboy organizations over the past few years, and I'm sure all of South Amboy and Sayreville will be rooting for his continued success. Good luck, Jack!

McKeon's Marlins Visited Mets At Shea Stadium

By Tom Burkard

(Article appeared in the July 26, 2003 issue of *The South Amboy-Sayreville Times*)

I had the pleasure of visiting South Amboy's favorite son, Jack McKeon at Shea Stadium June 24-26, when his young and talented Florida Marlins baseball club invaded New York to take on the Mets in a three-game series.

McKeon, who has been cast in the role as a modern-day miracle worker, has been doing just fine. Since taking over the manager's post from Jeff Torborg on May 11th, his club reached the .500 mark on June 24th with its victory over New York. It was quite an accomplishment, considering that when he was hired, the Marlins were six games below .500.

Florida is a very young team, but has plenty of talent, and McKeon is a perfect fit for patiently guiding the youngsters as they continue to develop on the major league level. Jack has an excellent rapport with the entire team, and it is evident by the way he interacts with the players, giving them friendly advice in a one-on-one basis. They certainly appreciate his help, and you can tell that they really respect him. The Marlins have a relaxed atmosphere in the clubhouse and on the field during batting practice. There is no doubt that Jack McKeon is the person responsible for bonding this young group into a baseball family.

In an exclusive *South Amboy-Sayreville Times* interview in the manager's office before the series opener against the Mets, Jack told myself, and New York's legendary sportswriters, Red Foley and Jack Lang, that his Marlins are "In a good place. We'll finish over .500 and make it interesting."

It was definitely an interesting little group we had there, discussing baseball, and for me just getting to listen to these ultimate professionals. McKeon, who has been in pro baseball for over 50 years, along with Foley and Lang, two of New York City's greatest sportswriters in history, with over 50 years each of outstanding journalism!

Lang mentioned to McKeon that Dan Castellano had some health problems and would miss Jack's team for the first time ever on their trip to New York. McKeon concerned for his old friend, immediately asked Lang for his phone number, and said, "I'll have to give Dan a call. He's a great guy." Castellano was one of the top sportswriters in *Star Ledger* history.

I asked Jack about his ace rookie pitcher, Dontrelle Willis, and he said, "He's colorful with a lot of charisma, and fun to watch." The media demands have been great on Willis, who upped his record to a lofty (8-1) after beating the Mets in the rubber game of the series. McKeon, who has taken Willis under his wing, said, "I have to monitor the press for Dontrelle. I told him to put it into focus."

In addition to Willis, the Marlins have other fine players who are having big years. Third sacker, Mike Lowell has blasted 28 home runs, while center fielder, Juan Pierre tops the NL with over 40 stolen bases. Last year's stolen base king, Luis Castillo is batting near the .310 mark. Ivan Rodriguez, future Hall of Famer is the superb catcher, and has his average over .300. He also blasted a big home run against the Mets.

McKeon is well aware and appreciates the talent on his club, and only wishes that they could all get to play in the All-Star Game. "I'd like to see about five of my players on the All-Star team," he said.

Jack is still in demand when it comes to interviews, and when I arrived at his office in Shea Stadium on June 24th, it was filled with local and national media firing questions at the Marlins' skipper. When we went onto the field for batting practice in the 100 degree heat, he was interviewed on radio and TV. Nothing stops this energized, 72-year young dynamo. When reminded that he's the third oldest manager in baseball history behind Connie Mack and Casey Stengel, McKeon responded, "I'm the oldest guy to be hired in any sport."

McKeon told me that he lost 30 pounds, mainly by jogging every day at the ballpark, wherever his team is playing, and sticking to a strict Atkins Diet. It really is paying off. He looks great!

The Marlins' coaching staff features three of the nicest pros I've ever met. Bill Robinson, Ozzie Guillen and Jeff Cox are all down to earth, good people. I also had the chance to talk to Florida players, Pierre, Rodriguez, backup catcher Mike Redmond, and the nicest, most mannerly of all, young Mr. Willis.

The energized Jack McKeon and his Florida Marlins are starting to liven up the 2003 baseball season. These kids can really play ball, and McKeon is certainly the master manager, so keep your eyes on the Marlins in the second half.

On July 6th, Jack won his 800th career game, as his club swept Philadelphia in three games. He became the 63rd manager in history to accomplish this great feat. Ironically, he won his 300th and 500th games against the Phillies.

As of July 8th, Florida's record was 31-22 under McKeon, since he took the managerial reins on May 11th. Since May 23rd, the Marlins were 28-15, the best record in the NL East.

Ivan "Pudge" Rodriguez and McKeon flash winning smiles at Shea Stadium during the Summer of 2003.

Jack studies his superstar catcher, Ivan "Pudge" Rodriguez during batting practice in 2003 at Shea Stadium.

Legendary New York sportswriter, Red Foley (r) jokes with his old buddy, Jack McKeon (l) at Shea Stadium in 2000.

Two of baseball's greatest managers, Jack McKeon (l) and Bobby Cox (r) of the Atlanta Braves.
(Photo courtesy of the Florida Marlins)

McKeon and leadoff hitter Juan Pierre are pictured prior to the start of another Marlins' game.
(Photo courtesy of the Florida Marlins)

How Sweet It Is! Jack smoking his victory cigar after defeating the Yankees for the World Series Championship in 2003. His wife Carol is very proud of her husband of 50 years.
(Photo courtesy of the Florida Marlins)

.Jack McKeon (r) gives Juan Pierre a high-five after the talented center fielder comes through again for Florida. (Photo courtesy of the Florida Marlins)

*2003-Jack (l) visits with his long-time friend, Jay Horwitz, who is the
Vice President, Media Relations for the New York Mets.*

*Ozzie Guillen (r) pictured with
McKeon (l) was the Marlins'
third base coach in 2003. He
was hired as manager of the
Chicago White Sox for 2004.*

ESPN's Jeff Brantley (r) interviews Jack in 2003. Brantley was a former major league pitcher.

2003-Two of Major League Baseball's finest managers, Art Howe (l) of the New York Mets and Jack McKeon (r) of the Florida Marlins pose for a great photo at Shea Stadium.

Jack visits with legendary New York sportswriter, Jack Lang in 2003.

The 2003 National League "Rookie of the Year," Dontrelle Willis (r) poses with skipper Jack McKeon during the Summer of 2003.

2003-McKeon (c) has a pre-game chat with pitching coach Wayne Rosenthal (l) and bullpen coach, Jeff Cox (r).

McKeon (r), known for his excellent handling of young pitchers, gives a few tips to Brad Penny (l) in 2003.

Jack (r) receives an award of appreciation from his cousin Jay McKeon on behalf of the Protection Fire Company in South Amboy. The presentation was at Veterans Stadium in Philadelphia in September 2003. (Photo by Brian Stratton)

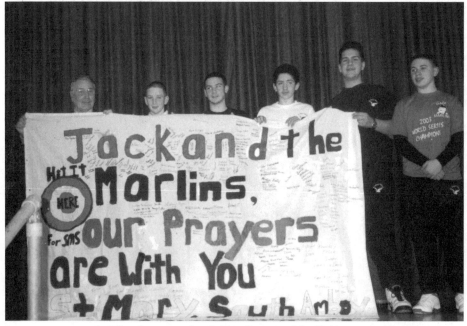

Jack (l) and youngsters from St. Mary Elementary School hold up a sign which they made and sent to McKeon in Florida for the World Series.

Cardinal McCarrick High School in South Amboy, formerly known as St. Mary's, which is McKeon's alma mater, shows its pride for its native son.

St. Mary's Elementary School in South Amboy also had a congratulatory sign after the Marlins won the World Series.

Carol (l) and Jack McKeon (r) make a perfect couple at the huge Tribute/ Dinner held in his honor on January 23, 2004 at St. Mary's School Gym. The couple celebrated their 50th Wedding Anniversary on October 29, 2004.

Jack McKeon (2nd from right) with family following the Tribute/Dinner in January 2004.

146

A Routine Florida Day In 2003 For Marlins' Manager

Marlins' manager, Jack McKeon told us his regular daily routine when his club is playing at home. "My routine day starts when I get up at 7:45 a.m., go to church at 8:30, and then to the ballpark. I walk or jog five miles, sit in the sauna for about 30 minutes, and then sit by the Jacuzzi. Then I'll go in the bullpen and smoke a couple of cigars, read the papers, make some phone calls, and get ready for the team to come out around 5:00 p.m.," he said.

McKeon Talks About Returning In 2004

(In an interview at Shea Stadium in September 2003)

I asked Jack, 'Will you be back next season?' He responded: "We'll talk at the end of the season. Some days I want to come back, some days I want to spend time with my family. I made a commitment to stay to the end of the season. A lot could depend on how things work out the last couple of weeks of the season."

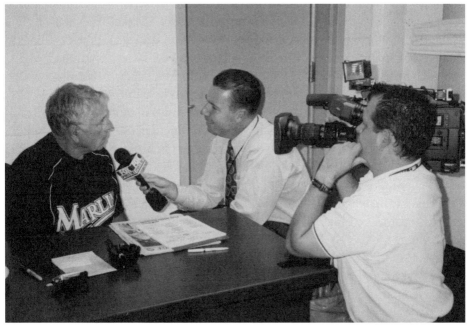

Jack McKeon (l) is shown during a pre-game interview with Fox Sports New York television's award-winning broadcaster, Matt Loughlin (c). Matt graduated from the same high school as McKeon.

McKeon's Magic Takes Marlins To World Series

By Tom Burkard

(Article appeared in the October 25, 2003 issue of *The South Amboy-Sayreville Times*)

"They said it couldn't be done," was a phrase used in a popular TV ad in the 1960's, and it was also the sentiment of many sportswriters throughout the U.S., who said the Florida Marlins were crazy to hire a 72-year old manager to handle their very young ballclub this year.

Well, the doubting scribes and sportscaster, Rob Dibble all had to eat their harsh words, as South Amboy native, Jack McKeon guided his Marlins baseball club to the National League Championship, by coming back from a two game deficit, to defeat the Chicago Cubs, 4 games to 3, and win a shot at the New York Yankees in the World Series.

McKeon, who had won several championships as a minor league manager, got to MLB post-season for the first time in his 50-plus years in pro ball.

Jack has become baseball's "most exciting story" of the 2003 season. He was home in North Carolina for the last two years, and a routine day for him consisted of attending daily Mass, riding his tractor, working out at the YMCA, and watching his grandchildren competing in different sports. He also kept up on the world of baseball by watching it as much as possible on TV.

Then the call came from the Florida Marlins front office, and the rest is history! Jack said his wife Carol was OK with him returning to baseball, because she could now have the TV set to herself. On May 11th, he took over as manager of the floundering ballclub, and critics sneered and joked about a 72-year old coming out of retirement to manage again. McKeon became the third oldest man to manage in the majors behind Connie Mack and Casey Stengel. He also became the oldest man to be hired in any major sports. At the time, the club had a record of 16-22, under Jeff Torborg, and was mired in fourth place, with the playoffs not even on their minds.

The first time McKeon met with the Marlins, he told them, "There's enough talent in this room if you want to work. You've done it your way, now do it my way. I want to be playing in October." He quickly changed the players' attitudes, and through patience and hard work, instilled confidence in the team, and made believers out of Florida, not just the ballclub, but the entire state!

The change didn't happen overnight, but McKeon seemed to be exactly what the young and talented Marlins needed to get them swimming in winning waters.

I had the opportunity to cover the Florida team for six games at Shea Stadium and one (the day of the hurricane) at Veterans Stadium in Philadelphia. The Marlins' dugout and clubhouse is always laid back, with a relaxed-like atmosphere. Players are engaged in watching the game from the previous night on TV, playing cards, or just joking around and enjoying each others camaraderie. In the manager's office, McKeon answers hordes of questions by sportswriters from around the country. His coaches are all first-class guys, especially Jeff Cox (who played for Billy Martin at Oakland in the early 1980's), Wayne Rosenthal, the pitching coach (a teammate of Nolan Ryan's at Texas), Bill Robinson (former Yankee star), and Ozzie Guillen, third base coach (outstanding shortstop with the White Sox).

On the field during batting practice, everyone is all business and focused on their jobs and preparation for the upcoming game. Although, all the Marlin players are respectful, I personally found stolen base champion, Juan Pierre, rookie phenom pitcher, Dontrelle Willis, and star pitcher, Josh Beckett to be the most down-to-earth and friendly. When asked how they liked having Jack McKeon as their manager, they all said either "It's great playing for him," or "he is the greatest." Catcher, Ivan "Pudge" Rodriguez, a future Hall of Famer said that Jack is "The best manager I ever had." Another player stated that their skipper puts "Trust in them, and just lets them play."

McKeon may have mellowed a bit through the years, but demands that his players "be on time, and bust their butts on the diamond."

Jack was recently honored at Pro Player Stadium by AARP. As gag gifts, he received Viagra, laxatives, cigars, and a cane. He said, "I already had the cigars," and he certainly is telling the truth. The cigar is without a doubt, "Trader Jack's" trademark.

Age doesn't seem to faze McKeon. "Age doesn't mean a thing. I don't think of myself as old. I don't feel old," he said. He has stayed in better physical shape this season than men half his age. He lost over 30 pounds on the Atkins Diet, and by jogging everyday at ballparks wherever the Marlins are playing. He puts in five miles, and is totally dedicated to his conditioning program.

McKeon became the 12th manager in big league history to replace a fired manager in mid-season and guide his club to the playoffs. While under his outstanding guidance since May 11th, Florida racked up a superb 75-49 record and captured the Wild Card Playoff berth in the National League.

The fired-up Marlins, spearheaded by Rodriguez, defeated the defending National League champions, San Francisco Giants three games to one in the NLDS, and then copped the NL pennant over the Cubs. Jack said that, "Rodriguez is for real. He's something very special for us. We're fortunate to have him."

McKeon at 72 years old, and Giants manager, Felipe Alou 68, was a match-up of managers with the highest combined age in post-season history. Their total of 140 years was 12 years older than the combined ages of Casey Stengel of the Yankees and Fred Haney of the Milwaukee Braves who met in the 1958 World Series.

During my September interview with Jack in the Marlins' dugout at Shea Stadium, he spoke about some very interesting topics. He compared the '03 Marlins with the Reds team. "We're a much younger club than Cincinnati. This is probably the best club I ever managed as far as personnel. Plus, the attitude is tremendous! I never had a club that had so many good guys on it. No troublemakers whatsoever. We have a lot of youngsters who want to get better, and really are maturing."

When I asked what players were his biggest surprises, he responded, "Dontrelle Willis and Miguel Cabrera, our third baseman, who came up from Double A. A lot of young players have matured and developed since I've been here, and it's a big plus." McKeon said that his best team player-wise was the '99 Reds, with this Marlin club "close to it."

After winning the pennant over the Cubs, Jack said that, "People asked me if I was going to come back for next year, and I told them if I get in the World Series and get to manage the All-Star team, I'll definitely be back." That's great news for McKeon fans throughout the world!

In the Game 7 post-game interview, he said, "I really take this as a gift for my family, my wife of almost 50 years, who sacrificed so many things, my kids, my grandkids, through the years, never having a dad, a grandfather around. I'm happy for them. For the first time, they may be able to enjoy something special."

He said that, "The Cubs were always America's favorites. I think we're the darlings of the baseball world now." McKeon, a devout Catholic, who attends daily Mass, at whatever town the team is playing in stated that, "I've had a strong belief that we'd go all the way. I have a lot of faith in prayer. The good Lord has been looking out for us for the last month. I thank God for the great players. We love each other."

"Experts never predicted the Marlins to be near first place. They picked us for fourth or fifth. Everybody picked us not to be here, but this club has a lot of character. We're tough, and battle all the way. We don't quit. Our guys are full of confidence. They're just exciting to be around. They've got fire in their eyes. They're never going to quit. You're going to have to beat us," said the proud manager.

Star first baseman, Derek Lee said of the McKeon magic, "Jack has the Midas touch. Everything he does turns to gold."

Jack McKeon has captured the heart of America this season. He has proved that age is really "just a number" by taking over a team of young ballplayers, who were mired in a lackluster season, and turning them into bona-fide winners and champions.

Many South Amboy and Sayreville fans are rooting for McKeon's Marlins to defeat their beloved Yankees in the World Series. Congratulations, Jack on one super-stellar performance, and also the inspirational sports story of the year! You certainly get our vote for NL "Manager of the Year.

World Series-McKeon gives a big wave to his hometown newspaper, prior to the start of the 2003 World Series Game 2 at Yankee Stadium.

McKeon Mania Sweeps The Area

By Tom Burkard

(Article appeared in the November 22, 2003 issue of *The South Amboy-Sayreville Times*)

For local baseball fans, the month of October was the most exciting one in many years, as South Amboy native, Jack McKeon led his underdog , wild card Florida Marlins baseball club to the 2003 World Series Championship over the mighty New York Yankees.

It certainly wasn't an easy road for the 72-year old manager, who came out of retirement on Mother's Day in May to manage the young club, and from that point, compiled the best record in baseball, 75-49.

The Marlins fought hard to win the Wild Card spot in the playoffs, and in the NLDS, behind McKeon's strategy to intentionally walk baseball's greatest player, Barry Bonds, as often as necessary, defeated the Giants, three games to one. The "Miracle Marlins" then went on to shock the pitching plentiful Chicago Cubs and their "Home Run Deluxe," Sammy Sosa. Jack simply told his players during this run, "Let's have fun. Let's do the best we can, and fool the rest of the baseball world." After McKeon took the helm, "fun" became the key word for the Marlins, and he brought that missing element back into the picture. He made coming to the ballpark a joy and delight once again for the talented young Marlins' athletes.

Beating the mighty, and always fearsome New York Yankees was like David slaying Goliath. The Marlins had a three games to two lead going back to Yankee Stadium, and McKeon decided to go with young ace, Josh Beckett with only three days rest. Beckett said, "Jack is a fun guy to play for. He has a way of motivating you." The skipper's big gamble was questioned and criticized by baseball analysts and experts throughout the land, for not holding him back for a possible Game 7 start.

The young and highly talented Beckett rose to the occasion, and stopped the Yankees, 2-0, to give Florida its second World Series Championship. McKeon smoked thousands of cigars in his career, but none tasted better than the victory stogie he lit up at the clubhouse celebration. Totally elated, he said, "Beckett is special. That's why I started him on three days rest. He's got the guts of a burgular."

South Amboy and Sayreville are both huge Yankee fan bases, but during the World Series, many who know and love Jack had to root for him and his Marlins.

Notes & Quotes:

Approximately 40 local relatives, friends and fans from our area trekked to Florida for Games 3, 4, and 5 of the World Series. . .Jack was known as "Trader Jack" back in the '80's, when he was the Padres GM, but how about a new nickname? Maybe "Gambler Jack" for his brilliant gambles throughout the playoffs, and especially the controversial one with Beckett clinching the World Series in Game 6. . .Talking about Yankee Stadium, McKeon stated, "Yankee Stadium is the epitome of baseball. Seemed like they got to the World Series so often, you'd think there wouldn't be a World Series without them in it. Deep down in my heart, I was saying I want to play the Yankees because that's something special."

During World Series week, *The South Florida-Sun Sentinel*, Florida's largest daily newspaper sent a sportswriter to South Amboy for a feature story. He went to Foodtown, and in the article mentioned owner Ed Paczkowski Sr., his sons, Ed Jr., and Frank, workers Pat Martin, and Richard Lix. Pat spoke of her husband Larry Martin Sr., and son Larry Jr. The scribe also interviewed Marge Gorczyca (McKeon's sister), and Chester Gasiewski of South Amboy. . .

At 72 years old, Jack became the oldest manager to win the World Series, and also the oldest manager or coach to lead a team in any sport to a major national championship. . .

Marlins' owner, Jeffrey Loria rewarded his super-manager with a brand-new $95,000 Mercedes Benz black sports car. . .McKeon negotiated and signed a new contract for one-year. . .There have been countless praises heaped on Jack, but one of the best came from a Florida resident, who said, "Jack McKeon is a role model for senior citizens."

Quite a few locals attended World Series games at Yankee Stadium. Tom O'Connor of South Amboy was at Game 6 and said, "I'm happy for Jack. I'm a Yankee fan, but Jack's a great guy. I'm also happy for my father, Al O'Connor. He was Jack's teammate in high school, and Tom Kelly (managed Minnesota to World Championships in 1987 and 1991) played for my father's Enterprise Little Fellas League team in the 1960's."

Former South Amboy resident, John Kovaleski who now resides in Florida said, "Jack is considered the Messiah down here in Florida. Jack walks on water!"

Jack: Fan Friendly

(Prior to Game 3 of the World Series)

McKeon saw over 200 fans on line at the box office, waiting for tickets, and suffering in the scorching Miami heat. He walked down the line and shook everyone's hand, asking some "How you doing?" To others, he said, "Thanks for coming," or "Glad you're here" as well as exchanging other pleasantries. He also signed autographs. Not too many professional athletes would spend their time in the blazing Florida sun and socialize with the fans a few hours before a monster game like the World Series.

2003 World Series

Game 1	at	New York	Marlins 3	Yankees 2
Game 2	at	New York	Yankees 6	Marlins 1
Game 3	at	Miami	Yankees 6	Marlins 1
Game 4	at	Miami	Marlins 4	Yankees 3 *
Game 5	at	Miami	Marlins 6	Yankees 4
Game 6	at	New York	Marlins 2	Yankees 0

*(12 innings)

**Florida Marlins won World Series Championship, 4 games to 2 over the New York Yankees.

2003 National League Manager of the Year Voting

Jack McKeon, of the Florida Marlins, received 19 of 32 first place votes, and a total of 116 points from the BBWAA, to win the 2003 NL Manager of the Year Award. Chicago's Dusty Baker finished second with 62 points, followed by Atlanta's Bobby Cox with 56 points.

Third Best Sports Story of 2003: The Marlins

The Associated Press picked the Florida Marlins surprising World Series win as its third best sports story of the year for 2003. The Jack McKeon guided club received 121 first place votes, and a total of 536 points. The top story of the year was Kobe Bryant with 301 first place votes, and 616 points. Lance Armstrong, who won his 5th straight Tour de France title, notched 191 first place votes and 540 points, to take the second best story of 2003.

2003. . .What A Year!

It certainly was for manager Jack McKeon and his Florida Marlins. They finished 75-49, .604 winning percentage under him during the regular season. The men in teal then went on to beat the San Francisco Giants 3 games to 1 in the NLDS, and then the Chicago Cubs, 4 games to 3 in the NLCS. Florida capped a dream season, by defeating the New York Yankees, 4 games to 2 in the World Series.

Jack Said:

(About the 2003 season)

"I've enjoyed it very tremendously. It's probably the most enjoyable year I've ever had."

Friends and family turned out for Protection Fire Company's award presentation to Jack at Veterans Stadium in Philadelphia in 2003. (Phot by Brian Stratton)

On The "Late Show With David Letterman"

On November 5, 2003 McKeon was a featured guest on CBS TV's *Late Show with David Letterman*. He walked on stage with a big (unlit) cigar, and gave one to Letterman, who had become a father the previous day. Jack who was a laugh riot throughout his appearance, said as he handed the cigar to Dave, "Congratulations!" Letterman laughed and said, "And congratulations to you!" McKeon shot back, "I know what you're going through. I had the same problem." Letterman laughed and thanked him, and the crowd was in stitches.

The show's host asked Jack lots of interesting questions during his nearly 15-minute interview, ranging from the correct pronunciation of his name, to phenom Josh Beckett, as well as the Chicago Cubs fan who tried to catch a foul ball during the NLCS.

Early in the interview, McKeon gave his old high school a plug, mentioning that he had graduated from St. Mary's High School, South Amboy, New Jersey in 1948.

Letterman asked him how he pronounced his name, "Mc-Kee-on" or "Mc-Kyoon."

Jack responded, "I'm from the East, up here in New Jersey. Growing up it was Mc-Kyoon. People wanted to change it. I said, they can call Mc-Kee-on as long as they don't call me late for dinner." Letterman said, " I told Paul (Shaffer) you would say that."

When the Marlins hired Jack in May, many baseball experts scoffed at the idea, saying he was too old to manage, especially such a young team. Letterman asked McKeon how he overcame the age factor as a manager.

McKeon also tossed a good joke at Letterman, and the audience laughed hysterically. He said, "I had nine grandkids. You only got one-one child."

"I don't think that was ever a problem, Dave. I've had my greatest successes dealing with young players. Young players today are very receptive to picking up as much knowledge as they can. After four or five years in the league, they might be a little different," said McKeon.

Letterman said, "If our Yankees couldn't win, it was nice to see you have this victory." He then mentioned winning the World Series in Game 6 at nearby Bronx, and asked him what it was like because "It was you and a bunch of kids, essentially."

McKeon answered, "For our team, it was a great experience. A bunch of youngsters who had the best record in baseball since May 23. I managed all those years and never had a group of kids like this. We were very dedicated, very determined to win. When you think about it, they weren't awed by the playoffs or Yankee Stadium. Our philosophy of one game at a time carried over, and they didn't care if they were playing in Yankee Stadium or Woodbridge, New Jersey."

Letterman asked him, "Did you ever do anything drastic to get anyone's attention, someone who might have been a head case?

McKeon said, "There was one situation back in 1960. I was managing in the Carolina League, in Wilson, North Carolina. I had this Cuban boy, Juan Visteur. I'd be coaching third, and he'd be running the bases and come around third, I'd try to hold him up. 'Bing' . . . out at the plate. Next week, 'bing'. I said, 'Look, next time you do that I'm gonna shoot you.' We went to Elon, North Carolina the next day, and in the window of a pawn shop, I saw blank guns for sale,

$3.95. I got blank cartridges. I waited, knew it was gonna happen again. He's on second, ball hit up the middle, second baseman knocks it down, I try to flag him down, he zings by me, I go 'pow-pow' six shots, he thought he was hit in the back. The next time, he scored, we never had any more problems."

McKeon continued, "I did that again in Denver." Letterman burst out laughing. Jack said, "Dave it works! I was managing Omaha, and we were playing in Denver. They had an exploding scoreboard, Burroughs and all those guys. My guys come up, Tony Oliva comes up, hits a home run, and nothing happens. I said, "I'll fix that tomorrow night. He hits a home run again, I get the gun out, 'pow-pow-pow'!

Letterman then went on to the subject of Beckett. "Beckett, what a cool customer," he said. "He's a special kid", McKeon said. "He's a youngster who has an extreme upside, he was an All-Star, and what a job he did for us stopping the Cubs. Great stuff. He really matured in that playoff series."

When asked what it meant to go up against Torre, "just a couple guys from the New York area who went all the way to the majors," McKeon responded, "Joe and I are friends. He's done a great job for the Yankees for years. The whole Yankee organization is good. Joe was happy this was the first time I had a chance to get to the big dance and finally win it. He said he was happy for me.

Letterman asked McKeon, "How about that foul ball in Chicago?"

"I felt sorry for the kid over there," McKeon said. "After all, the old saying is if a ball's in the stands, and the umpire signaled it was in the stands, we should let the fans have a chance to retrieve it. It's like you or I being up there. Only now that you got that new youngster, Harry, you're gonna have to work with those hands so you can grab it."

Jack as he appeared on "The Late Show With David Letterman" in November 2004.

Quotes and Comments By Jack McKeon...

(About Josh Beckett and his performance in Game 6)

"I said he could do it. A lot of people doubted it. This guy has got the guts of a burglar. He's mentally tough. I knew he had the confidence to do the job he did out there tonight.

****

(On coming back to manage in 2004)

"I just wanted to come back and see if we couldn't do it again. Whatever players they give me, I'll do the best I can. I know they'll do a good job in putting together the ballclub."

****

(About the players of today)

"Players are bigger and stronger. They're more intelligent than years ago. There are more college educated guys, and they're asking more questions and wanting more answers."

****

(On playing the Yankees)

"Yankee Stadium is the epitome of baseball. It seemed like they got to the World Series so often, you'd think there couldn't be a World Series without the Yanks in it."

****

(When questioned about pitching Beckett on three days rest)

"Historically don't mean a thing when you're playing the Yankees. If I had Bob Gibson out there on three days rest, would anybody be asking me how I pitch Bob Gibson? Nobody. That's the way we feel about Beckett."

****

(On being out of baseball from 2000 to 2003)

"I didn't retire. I was just unemployed for a while."

****

(On Age)

"You're only as old as you feel. Age is just a number."

****

(On Josh Beckett)

"I've had a lot of young pitchers, but believe me, this guy is by far the most outstanding young man I've had as far as mental toughness in the big leagues. I love that kid."

****

(When asked by media in late 2003 about his job status)

"If we make it to the World Series, I have to come back and manage the All-Star Game."

(On Josh Beckett before Game 2 of the World Series at Yankee Stadium)

"He's a great kid. He's a young kid and he likes to talk. We kind of agitate each other once in awhile. One thing about him is he may talk a lot, but he walks the walk as well. And that's what I'm so happy about."

****

(On the Marlins' defense)

"In my opinion, we have the best defensive all around club in the major leagues. I've never had a defensive club as good as this one."

****

(Talking about his first ride to the World Series)

"I really take this as a gift for my family, my wife of almost 50 years, who sacrificed so many things, my kids, my grandkids through the years, never having a dad, a grandfather around. I'm happy for them. For the first time, they may be able to enjoy something special."

****

(On Josh Beckett)

"He's just got that mystique that the great pitchers have. Every time he's on the mound, you feel you're going to win."

****

McKeon (c) makes a pitching change, as Dontrelle Willis' (r) work for the day is complete.
(Photo courtesy of the Florida Marlins)

McKeon Brings Hope, Inspiration And Love

By Tom Burkard

(Article appeared in the January 24, 2004 issue of *The South Amboy-Sayreville Times*)

The 2003 holiday season was history for just about a month, when one of the most world renowned figures returned home to South Amboy from January 22-25. Jack McKeon, who managed those fabulous Florida Marlins to a World Series Championship over the beloved New York Yankees last October, was back to where his "dream" all began in "The Pleasant Little City."

Major League Baseball's #1 Ambassador, honored his hometown by coming back to speak to students at the local schools, and much more which included attending two great parties, and three banquets, where he received a truckload of awards for his tremendous accomplishments.

The Jack McKeon "Jersey Tour '04" kicked off on Thursday, January 22nd, when he arrived at the South Amboy Middle/High School, and delivered a powerful talk to the youngsters about growing up in South Amboy and the burning desire he always had to become a professional baseball player. "I had a dream. I wanted to become a big league baseball player. In 1973, I reached my dream when I became manager of the Kansas City Royals. Then, I set my sights on another goal. I wanted to make it to the World Series," he said.

During his rookie year in '73, the City of South Amboy held a "Jack McKeon Day" at Yankee Stadium, and he recalled his mother leaning over and whispering to him that "your dad would have been so proud of you." Jack said that "I always wanted to make my parents proud, and never embarrass them." He told the students to, "Go home and give your parents a hug, and tell them that you love them. Hug your teachers and tell them that you love them. Thank all of your coaches."

The 2003 National League "Manager of The Year" hit home with a very sobering story about Alan Wiggins, an excellent base stealer, who was drafted by and starred for McKeon when he was GM with the San Diego Padres. Wiggins, who died from AIDS related to drug use at age 32 in 1991, asked to see "Trader Jack" about two weeks before his death. "He didn't have courage to say no to drugs. He told me in the hospital to tell people the story of Alan Wiggins," said McKeon. The students sat and listened attentively, as the big leaguer's words impressed upon them the dangers of drugs.

"Your attitude determines your altitude. I picked my friends who had the same determination. There were guys who were doing drugs and drinking, and running around, but I avoided them and hung around with guys like me, who wanted to succeed," stated McKeon.

He continued, "It's not enough just wishing to make your dreams come true.

160

You have to study hard, say no to drugs and alcohol, work hard, be persistent, and have a good attitude. "Combine all of those together, and your dreams will come true like they did for me."

The 73-year young manager, third oldest in major league history behind the legendary Connie Mack and Casey Stengel, was a huge success and blasted a grand slam home run at the first stop on his goodwill tour. After the lecture, students mobbed him for autographs outside the theater, where he signed at least 100 in about a half hour, and posed for photos with teachers and school officials. Everyone apparently realized that they had been touched by greatness, and wanted a souvenir to always remember their big day with Jack McKeon.

Next stop was the South Amboy Elementary School, and most of the younger children were proudly wearing teal colored, Jack McKeon tee shirts. Far more vocal in their support than the older students, they cheered and applauded throughout McKeon's presentation at the old High School Gym on George Street.

On Thursday evening a private party was held for Jack at the Enterprise Fire House on George St., with family and close friends in attendance. He received several awards from the City of South Amboy, The Emerald Society of Middlesex County, and other organizations.

Thursday was pretty busy, but Friday was even more fast-paced for the energized McKeon. He started the morning off with a 9 a.m. assembly at St. Mary's Gym, where he spoke to all the students from St. Mary Elementary School, as well as the entire Cardinal McCarrick High School, which was formerly St. Mary's High School, where Jack graduated from in 1948.

The talk was once again very up-lifting and positive, and also left a lasting impression with the youngsters on how to achieve success, select good friends, and stay away from the evils of drugs and alcohol because they can prevent you from achieving your goals and succeeding in life. Immediately after the assembly, the Marlins' manager was picked-up on Stevens Avenue by a limo and driven to the airport to catch a private jet to Washington, DC, to assemble with his World Champion Florida Marlins team and meet President Bush at the White House. Following his afternoon in Washington, DC, he flew back to New Jersey, and made it to South Amboy in plenty of time for the Tribute/Dinner at St. Mary's Gym.

Prior to the big, hometown event, I visited with Jack and Sister Esther Hernandez, and he proudly showed us a new pair of rosary beads he received from Florida owner, Jeffrey Loria on the way to the White House. "Mr. Loria got them from a friend who had just returned from an audience with the Pope. The rosary beads are sterling silver and were blessed by the Pope," said McKeon.

Almost 400 people came out to honor Jack and his family. Mickey Gross was the co-chairman of the Tribute/Dinner Committee, and also did an exceptional job as Master of Ceremonies of the event. McKeon posed for photos with almost everyone, and signed over 500 autographs throughout the evening.

Jack received nine awards and proclamations including: "South Amboy Irishman of The Year" from the Ancient Order of Hibernians; A special award from the South Amboy Police Dept.; An award from the Emerald Society of Middlesex County presented by Chairman Pete Kenny; Other awards were from Cardinal McCarrick High School-High School Staff; St. Mary's Grammar School-Faculty; St. Mary's Athletic Association-Athletes of the Association. McKeon received proclamations from: New Jersey Senate and Assembly-Assemblyman John S. Wisniewski and Senator Joseph Vitale; Middlesex County Freeholders-Stephen Pete Dalina; City of South Amboy-Mayor John T. O'Leary.

Pete Kenny, Chairman of the Middlesex County Emerald Society, announced "Ladies and gentlemen, welcome to the house that Allie Clark built" (Referring to St. Mary's). MC Mickey Gross then introduced Allie Clark as "Mr. Baseball of South Amboy," and the PA system blared out the classic song, "We Are The Champions," a 1977, #4 hit by Queen.

Clark, South Amboy's first major leaguer, received a standing ovation when he took the stage to introduce Jack. He praised and congratulated McKeon for all of his great accomplishments, and also how he never forgot where he came from.

McKeon, praised Clark, as he had done at all of the events throughout his four day tour. He said that "Allie was an inspiration. We all wanted to emulate him when we were kids. He paved the way. He showed us the way. I appreciate it, Allie."

McKeon continued to praise his Marlins' for winning the World Championship: "I had a good bunch of players, and they made it happen." His modesty is highly commendable, but any baseball fan knows that Jack McKeon was the skipper responsible for steering the Florida baseball ship to the title. With over 50 years of experience in the game, and a master at baseball strategy and handling personnel, he was probably the main ingredient for "The Year of The Marlins."

Jack also thanked the audience for the hospitality, support and love they gave him through the years, and said, "South Amboy will always have a place in my heart."

Patricia Cahill, Principal of St. Mary's Grammar School gave the closing remarks.

The event was a major success, and everyone raved about Jack's friendly and down-to-earth personality, and how happy they were to either have gotten his autograph or had their pictures taken with him.

On Saturday, he was a featured guest at a sports memorabilia show at the

Meadowlands. Also signing was Paul Molitor, recently selected to the Hall of Fame, and former Yankee legend Joe Pepitone. Jack signed over 800 autographs in a couple of hours. He also filmed a "Halls of Fame" show with Mets sportscaster, Fran Healy, who played for McKeon at Kansas City.

That evening, Marge Gorczyca, Jack's sister threw a private party at her home in South Amboy for family and friends. There was still some more autograph signing to do for the popular McKeon, and then we finally got a chance to sit down and do an exclusive interview.

The last day of Jack's tour was another memorable one, starting off with the New Jersey Sportswriters Association's 68th Annual Banquet at The Pines in Edison. In the V.I.P.Room prior to the banquet, Jack was the most sought after celebrity for interviews and photos with the media. Other big names in attendance were Basketball Hall of Famer, Walt "Clyde" Frazier, Sparky Lyle, Joe Borowski, Jerry Cooney, Tom Glavine, Ken Daneyko, former Governor Brendan Byrne, and organist, Eddie Layton.

McKeon received the "Man of the Year" Award and also "Manager of the Year Award" from the New Jersey Sportswriters Association. He gave a fine speech crediting his team for the great 2003 season, and also thanked his family and friends for their support. He concluded by saying, "Here we are winning the World Series, and as Ray Kroc (Former owner of the San Diego Padres) said, 'Dreams do come true,' and I believe him now."

Jack McKeon's four-day visit was an incredible one I will never forget! He went out of his way to visit not only the Catholic schools he attended, but also the public schools, spreading positive messages to the youth about how to lead a good, wholesome and successful life, while staying away from the evils of alcohol and drugs.

In addition, wherever he went, he brought smiles to young and old alike. Whether it was by a simple handshake, a "Hello, how ya' doin," or signing his autograph, he touched people in such a beautiful way, and brightened up the day, like a bright sun shining on a harsh New Jersey winter.

McKeon is a modest man, who does not advertise all the goodness he brings into the world. I found out a story about a good friend of Jack's, a priest, who had season tickets to the Marlins' home games. Jack asked him if he was coming to the World Series, and the priest said he couldn't afford the tickets. McKeon went out and bought the tickets for the priest, and called with the surprise to tell him he had tickets for him. The priest was so moved by Jack's act of kindness, that he broke down in tears.

Going back to his days at San Diego, he got involved with a league for disabled children, called the Challenger League. According to New York Post super sportswriter, Kevin Kernan, who was working in San Diego at the time, "Jack would show up on Sundays and push kids around the bases in wheelchairs or just cheerlead and offer tips."

Thank you, Jack for a most memorable four days! See you in Spring Training!

Everybody's Talking About Jack

Mayor John T. O'Leary (South Amboy) "It was great that Jack came back to his hometown where he learned to play the game. It was really exciting for the children, and a very special four days. What impressed me most is his commitment to his family and community. This exemplifies the greatness in this individual."

Mickey Gross (Co-Chairman of Tribute/Dinner) "South Amboy should be very proud of the accomplishments of Jack McKeon. He proved what a World Champion he really is by taking time out to meet with the children of South Amboy. He has never forgotten his friends."

Gene O'Toole (South Amboy) "I thought it was a class act for him to come in and spend a day with the children at both high schools. He's a credit to his family and his faith."

Allie Clark (Former Major League Baseball Player, South Amboy) "I think it was wonderful. I think all the people of South Amboy really enjoyed seeing Jack. Coming back to his hometown means a lot."

Pat Cahill (Principal, St. Mary Elementary School) "It was great! His message to the children was really inspiring. He encouraged their religion and education. He spoke of accountability of children towards schoolwork and respect."

Pete Kenny (South Amboy) "It was nice of Jack to come to South Amboy. It was nice of his family and Marge Gorczyca to share him with us."

Ron Keegan (South Amboy) "He's a guy that didn't forget where he came from. He had a whirlwind tour. Everybody loved him."

Carol Galley (Principal, South Amboy Elementary School) "We loved Jack's visit! It was such a great experience for our kids to meet him personally. I told the kids that I have lived here all my life and never had the opportunity they had to meet him."

Dr. Patrick Martin (South Amboy Superintendent of Schools) "We were just delighted! He was such a gentleman. His messages were very inspiring, believe in your dreams and stay away from negative influences. He was originally going to speak at the Catholic schools, but they were most generous in the way they shared him. They had tee shirts made up, and brought him to our schools. They also shared the profits from the shirts with us. The two communities, public and Catholic schools came closer together. The students spent time with the manager of the champions, and the City of South Amboy became more unified. It was so successful, that people are talking about the schools doing more and more activities together."

Dr. Frank Ianniruberto (Principal, Cardinal McCarrick High School) "Jack's visit was a very positive experience, particularly for the young people. He is a role model that exudes the attributes that if you work hard, believe in yourself and God, you can be the best person you can be."

Jose Aviles (Principal, South Amboy High School/Middle School) "It was a wonderful thing! He seemed like a humble individual. What impressed me most was that 40 or 50 kids surrounded him after his talk, and he signed autographs for every single one. He's pretty much an icon in South Amboy, a really nice guy. I appreciate that he came to the public schools."

Leo Kedzierski (Former St. Mary's teammate in the 1940's) "It was a great pleasure to see him again. I'm very happy for what he's accomplished. He set a goal for himself, and he did it. That's great! He's the same guy when we knew each other back in the 1940's. His talk to St. Mary's was fabulous!"

Leo Kedzierski (l) a former high school teammate of Jack's looks on as the 2003 National League "Manager of the Year" autographs baseballs for South Amboy's Kevin O'Connor.

Marlins Visit President Bush
At The White House

On January 23, 2004, the World Series Champion Florida Marlins were honored at a special ceremony by President Bush at the White House. Players and their families, and other members of the organization attended, as well as Florida Governor, Jeb Bush, Miami Mayor Manny Diaz, Marlins' club chairman, Jeffrey Loria, club president, David Samson, general manager, Larry Beinfest, and North Carolina congressman, Howard Coble, a friend of Marlins' manager Jack McKeon. A very proud and happy McKeon gave the president a cigar for allowing Coble to attend. Bush joked and said Coble and McKeon are "members of the old geezer club." He also said that "McKeon is the Donald Rumsfeld of baseball. He's kind of crusty, but knows what he's doing."

Jack McKeon shares a joke with President George W. Bush at the White House on January 23, 2004, when the World Champions were the guests of the President. Other members of the Florida Marlins' family enjoy the moment. (Photo courtesy of Florida Marlins)

McKeon's Speech At 2004 Tribute/Dinner

On the evening of January 23, 2004, after spending the day at the White House in Washington, DC with President Bush, Jack McKeon returned to his hometown in South Amboy, NJ. He was honored by the City with a gala

Tribute/Dinner, attended by over 400 locals. The following is the speech he delivered at St. Mary's School Gym:

"Allie Clark, the first major leaguer from South Amboy, showed us the way. Allie paved the way. When he continued to have success on his rise to the big leagues, for me, my brother and the O'Brien Twins. He was the inspiration. He was paving that road. He showed us the way. I appreciate it, Allie!

So many people played a part in helping me have a little success, and you go back and take a Gene Thomas, the old scout, who used to live on Louisa Street, next to my father's garage, and how he used to come out on his porch and talk baseball all day to us. We'd go down and sit at the South Amboy Trust Company Bank and talk baseball. That was remarkable! Then you go back to Richie Ryan our high school baseball coach, Bob Eppinger, Reggie Carney, "Red" Connors, the guys that coached us in basketball. They all made contributions and helped us along the way. There is some little part of those guys in us today. Chet Meinzer when we were Little Leaguers, Joey Crowe, "Mike" Carroll, Bill Stratton, former professional and semi-pro players. They always encouraged us and helped us along the way. They tried to instruct us and put us in the right direction. "Doc" O'Leary, "Utzie" Schultz. "Doc" always found a team for us to play. "Utzie" Schultz always made sure we got to all these things. My parents, how much they provided for us, all the necessities and encouraged us never to give up. The coaches in high school that worked their tails off, and cared for us, and made it exciting and showed us the right way to do things. I'll always be grateful. South Amboy will always be special in our hearts.

30 years ago when in my first Major League job in Kansas City, the big thing in my mind was, here I am a young guy 42 years old dreaming of winning a World Series, and hopefully it would happen in New York where all my friends would get an opportunity to come. And after many stops along the way, I've had some ups and downs, I continued to be persistent and was still trying to follow that dream. But, when I was let go by the Reds in 2000, I thought it was the end of the line. At my age, who's gonna hire an old goat? I thought that I might stay in baseball, but never manage in the big leagues again. My dream was unfulfilled. And, I remember Ray Kroc, owner of the San Diego Padres always preaching to us 'persistence was the key to success,' and that 'dreams do come true." For two years, I laid out, and watched my grandkids play sports, and I was getting tired of watching soccer, but anyway, I got the itch and I go to church everyday. I have a favorite saint, Saint Theresa, Prodigy of Miracles. I'd say a few prayers to her once in awhile. I'd say to her how about talking to the big Man upstairs and see if there's someone around that wants to take a chance on an old goat. Well, 1 1/2 years later, I get that phone call, and there I am. It's from the Florida Marlins. I'm getting that one more chance I wanted.

An SA Times Exclusive Interview With "Manager of The Year," Jack McKeon

By Tom Burkard

On January 24, 2004, I finally caught up with the much-in-demand 2003 National League "Manager of The Year," Jack McKeon. This is at least the sixth exclusive interview we've done since 1999, and I must say that Jack is getting more interesting, and humorous every time we meet.

We discussed a large variety of topics both past and present, and I really don't believe that there is a nicer, more sincere person in all of major league baseball. Believe me, I should know. I've had the opportunity to meet about 300 big leaguers, and none come close to the South Amboy born and bred McKeon.

Although the Marlins lost eight players from the championship roster, with the most important one being the great team leader, Ivan "Pudge" Rodriguez, manager McKeon is optimistic about the upcoming season. "Spring Training will be interesting. We have a lot of new faces. It will be a lot of hard work, and hopefully, we'll motivate these guys to realize that it's going to take a lot more effort this year. It's not going to be handed to us. Everybody's going to be shooting for us. We're going to keep our starting pitchers intact, and with the addition of A.J. Burnett, we're going to be in good shape again. He should be ready by May 15th."

Jack feels the Marlins' attendance should be good, as long as the club is successful. "Winning is the key to everything. I think initially they'll come out, and if we keep winning, they'll support us," he said.

How does he feel about Florida's chances to repeat as World Series Champions? "It's always going to be tough to repeat. You haven't seen many clubs repeat except for the Yanks a few times, but they haven't done it lately. With the way the game is today, and everybody switching over changing clubs and changing leagues, free agency, arbitration, it's tough to keep teams together," he stated.

When asked if this off-season was the busiest in his 50 plus years in pro ball, he quickly replied, "No question about it. When you win, you got all these functions you're obligated to attend. I didn't get as much time to spend in New Jersey as I'd like to. I guess that's the price you pay when you win."

He said his highlights over the winter were meeting President Bush, visiting the schools in South Amboy, getting the "Irishman of the Year" award, and the day long parade and "Jack McKeon Day" in North Carolina. "It's always special to be honored. It makes you feel it's a celebration for the hometown for what you've achieved. It's good for the community. All the old friends come out of the woodwork. We're all back there, seeing each other, having get-togethers and reminiscing. It brings back good memories of the good times we had in South Amboy."

I asked Jack what it was like to win both the World Series and "Manager of the Year" award in one season, and he responded, "It's kind of special. A lot of times, it goes together, but with my situation, when I came in late, and didn't really win the Wild Card yet, and the voting was pretty close to being completed by the time we got in the playoffs, so it's a tribute from the writers and I thank them for it, for recognizing our job at an early stage."

McKeon and his Marlins got to meet President Bush at the White House, and said, "It was very interesting. We got a chance to see the Rose Garden and Green Room, statues and president's pictures. I had my picture taken with the president, and had a chance to kibbitz with him a little bit. I've known him because he was in baseball (Texas Rangers), and we know a little bit about him. He knows the game and is very up on what's happened to me. I know his dad and mom better than I know him. I've had pictures taken with his parents, and now I got one with him. I know his brother Jeb, the Governor of Florida. He was at the White House too."

Many people considered the Florida Marlins World Series victory a "miracle." McKeon said, "I don't know if it was a miracle. I prayed to Saint Theresa Patron Saint of Miracles. My tribute goes to the players for their tremendous desire and determination. The price they paid to be successful and the resiliency they had. I owe it all to the players."

What about all those baseball analysts and geniuses who scoffed at the Marlins for hiring a 72-year old manager? "Age is just a number. I don't think you should penalize for experience and wisdom. All of us old guys, we've been through it. We made all the mistakes over and over. Now we're polished and know how to solve these problems. I think I set a new trend. All these guys, Gibbs, Whitey Herzog, Dick Vermil. Maybe ownership groups are realizing there is some value in hiring experience," McKeon stated.

What's it like to be admired and loved throughout the world for your great accomplishments? "It's a great feeling, really to be supported and loved by many people of Florida and here. My religious values with the Catholic Church have gotten a lot of publicity, and I've been getting so much mail about Saint Theresa from nuns, priests, fans, and senior citizens writing me letters that I've inspired them. Not only by my religion, but by my work ethic and workouts. I'm trying to get seniors to realize you've got a life to live. Live your life! Don't sit in a rocking chair and rock yourself to death. Get out and get a life! Get moving," Jack said.

McKeon is looking forward to managing the National League All Stars this July. "This will be the topping on the cake. Basically, I've done it all. We went to the World Series for the first time, and now I'm getting the opportunity to manage the All Star Game. I've won the pennant, World Series, and now I'm going to the All Star Game," he said.

The word was out that when Jack played in the minor leagues, he tried switch-hitting. I asked him about it and his response was hilarious. "I hit righty and lefty. Well, I hit three ways really. Righty, lefty and seldom." Well, when it comes to managing, Jack McKeon bats 1.000 in my book!

Jack Said:

(During the off-season, 2003)
"I think we'll have a winning team next year."

2003 National League Manager of The Year Award Presentation

On January 25, 2004 at New York, Jack McKeon received the 2003 National League Manager of the Year Award at the BBWAA annual awards banquet. New York Mets manager, Art Howe presented the award.

Howe said, "No one deserves this more than Jack. He worked very hard. He used his enthusiasm, his knowledge and his insights to guide a young team to the World Series Championship."

Jack's speech was humble, yet laced with plenty of humor that had the crowd laughing hysterically. He said, "I'd like to congratulate all the award winners. It's an outstanding group of men. I could use a few on my club next year.

"I'm so glad to see them give out plaques. I remember once, many years ago, I was with the Atlanta Crackers, and on my way home from getting an award from the local Police Boys Club, I ran a red light. I was naturally stopped, and I explained to the officer where I'd been and showed him the plaque I received. Well, by the time he finished telling me what I could do with that plaque, I was so glad I didn't get a trophy," he joked.

"And Roger (Clemens) over there. . .that game in the World Series, we're all applauding him. I was going to take the tape of that game and frame it, and tell my great-grandkids, 'Yessir, I saw his last pitch.' Well, he sure screwed me up there," he kidded. The crowd loved it!

Jack Said:

(In a January 24, 2004 interview) "A few of the greatest players in the game today in my opinion are: Barry Bonds, Alex Rodriguez, Roger Clemens, Randy Johnson, and Pedro Martinez, and that's just a few."

The 2004 Baseball Season Interviews, Quotes, Events And Much More. . .

McKeon's 2004 Managing Philosophy, As Compared To 1973

How does Jack McKeon's managing philosophy differ in 2004 from when he was a major league rookie manager in 1973? Jack discussed it at Spring Training 2004.

"I'm more patient now, and I don't let little things bother me. When you first come to the big leagues, you wanna impress somebody. Every little thing bothers you. You want everything right. Now you don't see a lot of things. You don't hear a lot of things. You just don't let the little things bother you."

Jack Said:

(On his philosophy on managing)
"Have fun. If you have fun, you win, and winning is fun."

Did You Ever Wonder?

What players go where for split squad games in Spring Training? How is this determined? Marlins' manager, Jack McKeon explained it in March 2004 at the club's Roger Dean Stadium.

"You gotta have four of your regulars on the field at all times. So in split squad games, you split them up the best as you can. Take your three outfielders that are regulars and put them on one team with a catcher. Then take your four infielders and starting pitcher. As long as you take a total of four, that's the rule. Sometimes, where the game is played determines who you send. I kind of lean on giving the veterans a break and not sending them on buses all the time.

I usually go to the game which at the time is most important to me. If there's somebody I wanna see. If we have a home game or a road game, I'm staying at the home game."

Retirement? Not In Jack's Deck of Cards

In Spring Training 2004, I asked Jack, "After retirement, will you come back in some capacity to Spring Training?"

"First of all, I'm not going to retire. I may retire from managing, but I'll be involved. Like my present deal I have here with this club. I signed managing for one year, but also have a two-year deal that continues to ride every two years, and whenever I decide to pack it up, I'll stay on as an Executive Advisor for two years."

Jack Talks About Hitting Instructors

"I think the hitting instructors work with the players on an individual basis on hitting and to correct some of their flaws. I imagine they talk a lot of philosophy about the art of hitting. It's nice to have three guys around you that were pretty good hitters in their career. Perez is a Hall-of-Famer and Dawson is coming pretty close."

World Series Rings

The Marlins received their World Series rings on April 10, 2004 before their game against the Philadelphia Phillies at Pro Player Stadium. The pre-game ceremony delayed the start of the game by more than 30 minutes. The rings were brought to Miami in an armored Brinks truck from Calgary, Alberta, some 3,200 miles away.

The ring, designed by Owner Jeffrey Loria is without a doubt, the most exciting and spectacular of any championship rings in the history of professional sports. Loria worked with complete dedication in the off-season to design the rings. He began the task with 100 prototypes, and decided on a huge piece of jewelry with 229 diamonds, which includes a rare teal one to represent the eye of a marlin jumping through the team's logo, and also an unbelievable 13 rubies. Each ring weighed 3 1/2 ounces, and had such an incredible size that it allowed for the name, number and position/title of each player, manager or coach. Also printed on the ring is the team's regular season record (91-71), a picture of the World Series trophy, and results of each post-season series against the Giants (3-1), Cubs (4-3) and Yankees (4-2).

The retail price for the 14-karat white gold rings is approximately $40,000 each, but since Loria bought over 80, was believed to have paid in the $20,000 apiece price range. Loria called the rings "priceless," while manager Jack McKeon said that, "It's a very special day. After 50 years to finally get one, I'll enjoy it. It's a valuable piece of jewelry."

The Power of Prayer

Jack started the 2004 season off with his favorite saint, Saint Theresa in his back pocket again. He carries a small case of religious items including Saint Theresa rosary beads, a crucifix and a baseball angel. "I have a strong belief in the power of prayer, he said."

Jack is a devout Catholic who attends Mass everyday. He also has been known to mention prayer in his quotes to the news media. The following are a couple of his references to prayer:

(On his hope to manage again before getting called by Florida) "I was praying and praying that I'd get one more chance, that someone would hire me. . . But I didn't think anyone would take a chance on an old man like me."

(In 1998) "I went to church the other day to pray for our pitchers, but there weren't enough candles."

Jack Said:

(On playing in Puerto Rico in 2004)

"Playing in Puerto Rico is no different than playing in South Amboy, New Jersey or Lincoln, Nebraska. Actually, I like going to Puerto Rico. I have a lot of friends there from when I managed there.

Did You Know?

A radio station in Cincinnati wanted to have a parade for Jack McKeon for winning the World Series. "I said no way to that one. I'm not going there to rub it in," he said.

McKeon Wins 2,000th Game

Jack McKeon won his 2,000th professional game as manager on April 20, 2004, as his Florida Marlins defeated the Philadelphia Phillies, 3-1 at the Phillies' brand new Citizens Bank Park.

Left-handed pitching ace, Dontrelle Willis notched the victory, upping his record to 3-0, while running his scoreless string to 19 2/3 scoreless innings and a 0.00 ERA for 2004.

Willis hurled 6 2/3 innings, allowing one earned run on four hits with three strikeouts. Chad Fox and Armando Benitez combined for 2 1/3 hitless innings of relief.

Mike Lowell, Juan Pierre and Miguel Cabrera each had RBI singles to seal McKeon's monumental victory.

McKeon won 1,146 games in the minor leagues, and this victory was number 854 in the majors.

McKeon Interview at Citizens Bank Park
Home of the Phillies
April 21, 2004

Jack was as interesting, insightful and humorous as always during this early season interview in the visiting manager's office at the Philadelphia Phillies' brand new home.

I asked him questions on a wide variety of topics ranging from the good, old days to the present with his talented young Florida Marlins.

The Marlins won the previous night, and the victory marked McKeon's 2,000th win as manager in professional baseball. The strange thing was that none of the major sports media or networks even realized that Jack achieved such a monumental accomplishment. It wasn't mentioned at all, and this really surprised me.

So, needless to say, I asked him about his 2,000th victory, and he responded, "If it wasn't for you reminding me of it, I wouldn't have known. I didn't pay much attention to it. In this business for over 50 years, you don't keep up on all those records and keep track of them like it was only 200 or 300. When it gets to 2,000, you don't worry about them."

He did remember his first big league win though. "It was against the California Angels in '73, when I managed Kansas City. It was at the new Kauffman Stadium."

Jack was then questioned about Hall of Famer, Red Schoendienst, and he replied, "Red was a manager in the big leagues, and I hired him as a coach at Oakland in 1977, and he was my coach in '77 and '78 when I managed the A's. Red was a happy-go-lucky guy, good, knowledgeable baseball man. A guy that has so many friends in baseball. You just enjoy going out with him. He's an avid golfer. He's a real class gentleman."

McKeon also spoke about well-known baseball executive, Syd Thrift. "I worked with Syd for many years at the Baseball Academy with the Kansas City Royals, and he was my Advance Scout, when I was manager of the Royals. He was a guy I really respected his judgment on ballplayers. He was instrumental in getting a lot of key ballplayers for me when I was at Kansas City.

They were talking about George Brett, and I told Syd to go down (to the minor leagues) and see if he's ready to come to the big leagues, and if you tell me he's ready, I'll bring him to the big leagues. Syd said 'he's definitely ready,' so we got George Brett to the big leagues."

Another famous name, Johnny Sain worked for McKeon as a pitching coach. Jack said, "He's one of my favorites. I learned so much about pitching from him and Don Gullet. It was unbelievable the knowledge they had on pitching, and Johnny was recognized as a guy that didn't require his pitchers to do a lot of running, and his theory was 'They don't run the ball over the plate, they throw it over the plate.' I'd rather see them throwing than I would about the running. Sain was a guy that always believed in throwing everyday, as which the brave pitchers do today. He was a very successful and knowledgeable baseball man."

Jack worked for the interesting, late Marge Schott, who owned the Cincinnati Reds. "She was a good lady, a compassionate lady. She was misread by a lot of people. She shot from the hip, and told it like it was. She was like an old sailor in a barroom. When she was around friends, she just spoke her piece. A lot of times, she got in trouble because the media overheard her, and got something they could run with, and make a big issue. She cared very much for the Reds and her dog. They were her two loves. After her husband died, they were the only two loves that she had Schotzie the dog, and the baseball Reds. As far as an owner, she was one of the best I worked with. I had no problem with her, and really enjoyed working with her. She was a great gal.

Ray and Joan Kroc were the owners of the San Diego Padres, and McKeon was also employed by them. "Ray and Joan Kroc were outstanding people. They let you do your job. They were under the impression that they hired somebody to do the job, let him do his job. Basically, they stayed out of the way. I enjoyed my relationship with them tremendously," Jack stated.

We spoke about his younger days when he grew up in South Amboy, New Jersey, and who his favorite players were back then. He said, "I always tried to emulate Bill Dickey, DiMaggio, Phil Rizzuto, Tommy Henrich and those guys. I was a big Yankee and Giant fan when I was growing up, so I kind of remember all of those guys. I spent a lot of time watching them. I always followed the career of Allie Clark, and I've said many times that he was the inspiration to all of us in South Amboy, because we all wanted to be like Allie and get to the major leagues. He basically showed us the way. We followed his career on a daily basis, and I'm glad to see that he had a successful career. As we all know him now, he is one of the most outstanding gentlemen in the City of South Amboy."

Jack is well known for being a devout Catholic who attends daily Mass in whatever town his team is playing in. "I've been fortunate to find churches within 5-10 blocks of the hotels where we play. It's been pretty easy. If you search around, you can find them. In Philadelphia, when I first came here, I used to walk 15-16 blocks to go to church. I found there was one about a block and a half from the hotel. That's the one I go to now in Philadelphia. It's the oldest one in the country-St. Joseph's," he said.

McKeon always leaves a partially smoked cigar outside whatever church he goes into, because he can't smoke inside and doesn't want to waste it. He tells a funny story that recently happened. "Last week in Atlanta, I left one on the window sill, came out, and lost another one. It was gone! Atlanta is the most dangerous city I go into as far as losing cigars."

I wondered who his favorite manager of all-time was, and he said, "Danny Murtaugh. I played for Danny one spring at New Orleans, and we became pretty good friends. He was the one that recommended me to be a manager to Branch Rickey. He asked me if I ever thought about becoming a manager, and later recommended me to Mr. Rickey.

Even when I got to the big leagues, I used to call him and consult with him, and pick his brain. He was very helpful in those areas. Murtaugh noticed my managerial possibilities in 1953, when I was only 22 years old. Two years later, at 24, I started managing."

Does Jack have any stories about superstitious players to tell? You bet he does! "When I managed the Royals, every time Julio Gotay came to bat, he'd make the the cross in the dirt. So, I told my catcher that whenever he makes the cross, to wipe it out. He did it one day, and Gotay got pretty upset about it," commented McKeon. Incidentally, Jack said that he did not have any superstitions.

What does McKeon think of the Phillies brand new Citizens Bank Ballpark? "I think it's a real nice place, nice stadium. I think it's gonna be a hitter's park eventually. The fans have a great view from anyplace in the ballpark. It's very colorful, very clean, and I think it will be enjoyable for the fans of Philadelphia," he said.

Jack has been doing a radio and TV show on a regular basis for the Marlins this year. When asked how it was going, he said, "I do the TV show with Craig Minervini whenever we televise our games, and a weekly show with him as well."

McKeon was quite optimistic about his Marlins club this early in the season. He gave the following analysis, "We can't complain. We're not hitting like we can. We're getting outstanding pitching and keeping the opposition from scoring in most games. We played 13 games now, and the most we allowed was five runs Most of the time, if we keep them to three, we'll win. We know our hitting is gonna pickup. It's just a matter of time, if we can keep our head above water. We'll be all right.

Cabrera and Choi have helped us tremendously with power. Pierre hasn't been on base like we hoped, and Conine hasn't been hitting. Lowell and Cabrera have been doing most of the hitting so far. These guys are going to pickup. It's just a matter of time."

2004-Florida's new first baseman, Hee Seop Choi (l) poses with manager Jack McKeon (r) during Spring Training. Choi was traded to the Dodgers over the summer.

Jack-Always A Fan Favorite

In early May, 2004, after a routine early afternoon jog at Pro Player Stadium, Jack forgot his clubhouse key and pass. To kill time while waiting for the clubhouse attendant, the always friendly McKeon sat down under the statue of Don Shula, and enjoyed his trademark cigar, while kibitizing with fans.

Jack Wins 100th With Marlins

On May 24, 2004, Jack McKeon notched his 100th victory as manager of the Florida Marlins, as his club blasted Arizona, 13-5. Juan Pierre drove in four runs, and Ramon Castro three. Jeff Conine belted a home run, and Carl Pavano picked up the victory with seven strong innings. The win moved the Marlins into a tie with Philadelphia for first place in the NL East.

McKeon Talks About
Rookie Catcher Matt Treanor

Catcher Matt Treanor, in his 11th season of professional baseball, finally got the call to the big show from the Florida Marlins, and made his long-awaited debut on June 2, 2004. He was brought up from Albuquerque's Triple-A team to replace Ramon Castro who was placed on the 15-day disabled list.

Treanor made his first game a most memorable one, by starting against the Cincinnati Reds, and getting a single for his first MLB hit. Even more exciting for the youngster was catching 2004 NL Rookie of the Year, Dontrelle Willis, who had a perfect game for 6 2/3 innings until Sean Casey singled to break it up.

Manager Jack McKeon and Treanor had similar minor league careers. Jack was also a catcher for over 10 years, and played in 901 games with 2,799 at-bats. Treanor played in 890 games and had 2,744 at-bats before getting his promotion to Pro Player Stadium.

"He's a scrappy guy who puts the ball in play," McKeon said. "He brings a little life out there. He's tickled to be in the big leagues. He takes charge. Other guys have had the opportunities and didn't take advantage of it. They didn't hear Mr. Opportunity knocking."

Jack Talks About Inter-league Games, The All-Star Game, Bonds, Dick Allen and More. . .

The following interview took place on June 4, 2004 at Shea Stadium, during the Marlins first trip to New York since beating the Yankees in the World Series in October 2003.

Jack covered many topics and had some brilliant insights and ideas in regards to inter-league games.

When asked how he felt about managing the upcoming All-Star Game at Houston, he responded, "This is a special honor. The only way you get the honor is to win the National League pennant, which we did. I'll get a chance to manage all of these superstars and future Hall-of-Famers and All-Stars. It's going to be special. I've been there three times as a coach, in 1974, 1989, and 1999. I'm taking all my coaches, and I get a chance to select two managers, but we haven't done that yet."

McKeon has the highest respect and praise for the great Barry Bonds. "I think he's the best hitter in the game, no question about that. He may be the best hitter of all time with the way he has tremendous eyesight and tremendous hand-eye coordination. He doesn't swing at any bad pitches. He makes contact everytime, and he hits the ball hard everytime."

The subject of Roger Clemens and Mike Piazza being on McKeon's NL All-Star squad came up. Everyone remembers the confrontations the pair had back in 2000, but Jack sees no problem. "I don't know anything about that situation. I think they're both professionals, and if one is pitching and one is catching, I think they'll represent the National League very well, and their personal conflicts won't have anything to do with the outcome of the game."

Ken Griffey is having a tremendous comeback season this year, and I asked McKeon why Cincinnati Reds General Manager, Jim Bowden brought him to Cincy in 2000, and was it a wise move? The former Reds skipper said, "He was one of the all time great players and Bowden felt that this would be lent towards his legacy by bringing the biggest player in the game to Cincinnati. He's a good player, but he got hurt all the time. Now he's back this year as strong as ever and having the year we had hoped he would have had in 2000.

Bowden said that Griffey would make the difference in 10 games, but it didn't happen. It went 10 games the other way. Like I said, in all fairness to Griffey, he got hurt, and also the change in leagues didn't help."

In a May 2004 game against the Reds, McKeon opted to walk number 3 hitter, Sean Casey (who was leading the NL in hitting at the time), and pitch to Griffey. As fate would have it, Griffey blasted a game-winning home run, and as he rounded the bases shot a glare at his former manager McKeon. What about the glare, Jack? "I don't pay any attention to that stuff. When you look at it objectively, you say, hey the guy's a competitor. You don't like to get walked. You don't like to see the guy in front of you walked to pitch to you. It was a strategy move, it didn't work out. Naturally, he rose to the occasion and you gotta tip your hat to him and say, hey. Now as far as the glare, we've seen a lot of guys do that. It's typical competitiveness."

The creative mind of Jack McKeon went to work when he came up with a really outstanding theory on what should be done in inter-league games. "I didn't like it at first, but I like inter-league games now. The more I see how popular it is, the more I think it's nice for fans to see a different type of baseball. I suggest that we go to Cleveland and Detroit and let the pitcher hit, and when they go to Florida, they let the DH hit. It's so people could see the NL style in American League parks, and the AL style in National League parks."

McKeon said he likes the National League style of managing better than the American League. "In the NL, there are more switches to make. The strategy is different. In the AL, you stay with a guy, and don't have the double switches.

He talked about the Mets and Mike Piazza. "The Mets are an improved ballclub. I said in Spring Training that four clubs were in contention and can win our division. Cameron is a big plus for the Mets. He gives 100% all the time and wants to play." On Piazza playing first base, Jack said, "Give him some time. You can't expect him to be polished right off the bat. He's improved a lot since the last time we saw him. He's not doing bad over there. He's a good player. Yogi Berra played right field with a helmet on for the Newark Bears in '47. They didn't have a spot for him, but he became polished."

McKeon recalled the old days when he managed at Oakland. "When Dick Allen came to the A's, Charlie Finley told me to personally pick him up at the airport and set up the press conference. I put him in at DH in his first game, and he said, 'I ain't DH'ing. It's in my contract with Finley.' I had to pinch hit for him in the first inning," Jack said.

Another time, Earl Williams who was a catcher for the A's, but a better first baseman according to McKeon, replaced Allen at first base, and "Allen wouldn't come out. Now I got two first baseman out there," laughed McKeon.

Pete Rose made some comments in his recent book about Jack in regards to McKeon's treatment of Pete's son, Pete Jr. Jack said, "Well, I don't think he has any idea. I was the one that put his kid in the lineup and kept him in the lineup, hoping he'd get a couple of major league hits. Wherever Pete got that information was wrong. They (The Reds front office) told me when I brought him up to the big leagues, just to play him one game, let him hit one time, and get him out of there because he can't play. But, I stayed with him, but Pete didn't appreciate that, plus he didn't know about it."

Jack McKeon "Jack In The Box"?

On July 10, 2004, the Marlins held "Jack-In-The-Box" promotion prior to their game against the New York Mets. The first 10,000 fans received a giveaway Jack-In-The-Box, which features Jack McKeon popping out of a box with his arms outstretched and a cigar in his mouth. Of course, it was based on the idea of the original Jack-in-the-Box child's toy. The giveaway was sponsored by Tenet South Florida.

Jack said that the collectible was "A unique idea. You push the baseball button, and I pop out with a cigar."

Pittsburgh Wasn't Jack's Kind of Town

On July 18, 2004, after being swept in three games by the Pirates of Pittsburgh, skipper Jack McKeon said, "I'm glad to get out of Pittsburgh. We haven't won in three years here."

Jack Shows A Lot of Class

After Ken Griffey Jr. blasted his 500th home run, he received all kinds of congratulatory messages and accolades, but one that certainly surprised and pleased him had to be the one from his former Reds manager, Jack McKeon, whom Griffey played for in his first season with Cincinnati in 2000.

McKeon's message read: "Congratulations. You definitely are a Hall of Famer, and I'll see you in Houston at the All-Star game." This certainly showed that Jack harbored no ill feelings toward Griffey, and admired his contributions to the game of baseball.

The Reds of 2000 Could Have Been Like The Marlins of 2003

Jack McKeon has always felt that his 2000 Cincinnati Reds club was loaded with talent, and had enormous potential. In retrospect, he feels that, "If we went out and got some pitching and kept the club intact, I thought we had a chance. We had the great chemistry there, and I thought if they'd kept that club intact, we could have done what the Marlins did last year."

McKeon Picks National League
All Star Coaches

Jack McKeon, the 2004 National League All-Star manager chose managers Jimy Williams of the Houston Astros and Clint Hurdle of the Colorado Rockies as his assistants for the July 13th All-Star game at Minute Maid Park in Houston.

McKeon chose Williams because the game is in Houston, his home ballpark, and selected Hurdle because, "I wanted to give somebody a chance who hadn't been to an All-Star Game," he said.

McKeon's assistants representing the Florida Marlins will be, Jeff Cox (third base), Wayne Rosenthal (pitching), Doug Davis (bench), Perry Hill (first base), Bill Robinson (hitting), and Pierre Arsenault (bullpen coordinator).

In the 1999 All-Star contest at Fenway Park, Jack was chosen by San Diego's Bruce Bochy as an assistant coach, and was thrilled to be with the All-Stars and Ted Williams in the emotional ceremony in which Williams was surrounded by players from both teams, who came out to pay tribute to him.

2004 All-Star Conference Call

National League All-Star manager, Jack McKeon and American League manager, Joe Torre commented on several interesting topics at a national All-Star conference call.

After Torre answered a question pertaining to whether or not he would intentionally walk slugger, Barry Bonds, McKeon jokingly said that he might have Bonds leading off. Torre fired back again, kidding around, "You rotten thing. Well, there will always be a base open in the first inning, that's for sure." Jack gave the Yankee skipper something to think about when he said that, "Barry batted leadoff a lot of times when he with Pittsburgh. Well, it's food for thought."

McKeon stated that, "Barry is a tremendous player. He's the one guy in this game who can turn the game around any time at-bat, and I know people don't like to see the managers walk him, but we have a job to do as well. Our job is to win ballgames. He's probably the only single guy in baseball, who I can think of, who can beat you in so many ways. I think it's certainly a tribute to Barry for being such an outstanding player, that at times, he gets frustrated and the fans get frustrated as well, but I think all the managers show him total respect for his ability."

When asked about the distinct possibility of Roger Clemens pitching to Mike Piazza, and the type of scenario it may present, McKeon said, "I think both of those guys are professionals. We all have a purpose in Houston, and that's to win. I'm quite sure both of them are going to handle it very professionally."

Jack also spoke about his NL team, "I think every player on the All-Star team has a personal amount of pride. We're all going in with the idea that we want to win. I'll try to get as many players in as I can."

In the 2003 World Series against McKeon's Marlins, Clemens threw what was believed by everyone to be his final pitch in Major League Baseball. "I thought it would be the last time I saw him. I was tickled to death to someday tell my grandchildren that I saw the last pitch this future Hall-of-Famer ever threw, said McKeon.

The NL skipper also mentioned two of his All-Star pitchers, lefty Tom Glavine and Ben Sheets. He said that, "Tom Glavine is one of the top starting pitchers in the National League despite his record. He's been a victim of non-support in games he pitched against us. He's been selected by the players, and that's quite a tribute from his peers. He has proven in the past to be a successful major league pitcher."

"Sheets is one of the top starting pitchers in the league. He's up there in strikeouts and ERA. The times I've seen him on television, he's been exceptional," said McKeon.

On selecting Houston Astros' manager, Jimi Williams as his coach, Jack said, "He is an outstanding baseball manager and can help me in my first All-Star Game. He's been in a number of them."

McKeon feels that Carlos Beltran should play in the All-Star Game, even though he was traded from one league to another. "I think he's a great player and should be an All-Star. He certainly has the credentials to be on one of the All-Star teams."

The questioning went towards 500 home run hitters. "If anybody can hit 500 home runs, whether in Little League, college or whatever, they're worthy of being in the Hall-of-Fame," stated McKeon.

The National League will feature three players with 500 or more home runs in the same outfield for the first time in MLB history: Bonds, Sammy Sosa and Ken Griffey Jr. "I'm just delighted to be able to pencil those guys in the lineup. It's something to tell my grandkids. Hopefully, they'll get enough at-bats so they can do some damage to Joe's team," said McKeon.

How does Jack McKeon see the state of baseball this season? "I think it's the greatest game in the world. I think it's exciting. What we did in Florida last year has energized the game this year."

Jack, The All-Star Manager

As manager of the 2004 National League All-Star team, Jack McKeon became the oldest manager in history to guide a team in the Midsummer's Classic.

Jack and American League manager, Joe Torre of the New York Yankees, were guests on the TV show, *The Best Damn Sports Show.* McKeon said that, "I'm enjoying it tremendously. It's a great honor and thrill to be with so many great players in the clubhouse."

He also commented on two of his NL stars, Carlos Beltran and Lance Berkman.

"Beltran is a guy who was selected by the players in the American League, and all of a sudden, a few days later, he got traded. He has great numbers in the AL. When it all came down to weighing a number of factors, we thought he was a viable choice and deserving of being in the All-Star Game.

Lance Berkman has done an excellent job. I've seen him play center field. He was the next outfielder in the voting. I think he was very deserving to start the game in Griffey's place."

McKeon certainly appreciated the opportunity to manage in this game of baseball greats. "To me, the All-Star Game is a great exhibition. They're going to give it their best effort," he stated.

Everyone had a great time, but unfortunately his NL squad fell, 9-4, as future Hall-of-Famer Roger Clemens was shelled in the first inning by an awesome AL power display.

McKeon (r) poses proudly with Marlins' talented young slugger Miguel Cabrera.

Jack McKeon Interview
At Shea Stadium July 20, 2004

In yet another interview with Jack McKeon, we discussed an interesting variety of topics (As ususal).

When asked what the big difference was between the 2004 team and the World Champions of '03, Jack responded:

"Last year, we had a much different club. We had a Hall-of-Fame catcher in "Pudge" Rodriguez, All-Star first baseman in Derek Lee, and right fielder Juan Encarnacion, that gave us 68 home runs and 283 RBI, and the replacements this year haven't come quite close to doing that for us. That's the big difference in our club this year."

I asked Jack about Rodriguez, and he had so much praise for his 2003 team leader.

"He was the leader of our club. He was a very dynamic guy, an intense individual that was well-prepared all the time. He wasn't afraid to get on you if you weren't doing your job. That's something that goes with leadership. He was a great offensive force, but he was a guy that intimidated the opposition, and stopped their running game."

How was the All-Star Game?

"It was very exciting. You were able to pencil in all those All-Stars and future Hall-of-Famers, you know, Clemenses, Glavines, Sosas, Bonds' and the Rolens. It was great just being around all those guys and getting to know them a little better than you do when you see them across the diamond. Overall, it was something special. I spent a lot of time with my former Reds players, Larkin, Danny Graves and Sean Casey. Griffey wasn't there too much. (He pulled out of the Game because of an injury). We reminisced about the old days. It was a fun trip! The environment was great! All the All-Star Game festivities were something special. Watching all the 500 home run hitters and getting a chance to visit with some of them. It was pretty interesting.

The highlight for me was when I was announced as manager of the All-Star team. I've done everything in baseball now, so when I managed the All-Star team, I just about completed it."

A few days after the All-Star Game, McKeon was flown to Los Angeles to attend the ESPY Awards, in which he was nominated for "Coach or Manager of The Year." Jack said, "That's where they honored the top people in all sports. I was selected as one of the nominees for "Coach of the Year," along with Larry Brown and Bellichik of the Patriots and others. It was done by internet voting, and we were also nominated for "Team of The Year," and Beckett for "One Game Performance of The Year." It all turned out to be pretty good, but baseball didn't get any awards. They gave it to basketball, which is the last thing people remember. (Because the NBA finals had just ended). Baseball was way back in October, and people forgot about the baseball season. I thought the one award we should of got was for "Team of The Year." I don't think there was any more exciting team than what we did last year. Coming from nowhere and winning it. The Pistons were favored in their division and won it. The event was in L.A., and basketball was fresh in their minds, and they got the most votes."

What do the Marlins need to improve and get to the post-season again?

"We're gonna have to get our offense in gear. We can't keep scoring one or two runs in a ballgame, and expect to win a lot of games. We've got enough pitching, but it's a question of getting the offense going. At times, it looks like it's gonna get started, but it slips back. Lately, we haven't got the offensive support that we need. Hopefully, in the second half, we can generate a little more offense and make a deal to get a hitter that should help us."

Do you expect to recall any more youngsters from the minors?

"You're not going to be able to find Cabreras and Willis' every year."

Who do you think will be your toughest opponent down the stretch for the pennant?

"Honestly, I think it's a four-team division. The Braves because of their tradition, the experience they have, are gonna be tough. The Phillies probably have the best talent in the league. They're gonna be tough, and also the Mets. I think the Mets have tremendously improved. I think it's going

Jack goes over the pre-game scouting report in his office.

to be a question of who stays healthy and gets the best pitching near the end."

How was "Jack-In-The-Box" Day at Pro Player Stadium in Miami?

"It was great! It was very special! I happen to pop out of the box with a cigar. They had 41,000 at that game."

What was the Tampa Bay-Florida Inter-League series like?

"It's not like the Yankees and the Mets. We're on one coast. We don't have that kind of rivalry, even though we're intrastate. Piniella's doing good. They've got a good, young, interesting club. They're not ready to win it yet, but they've got a lot of young talent that's gonna be blossoming. I think in about another year, if they get some pitching, they're gonna be a World Series threat to a lot of these clubs."

2004-Jack (l) with his boyhood hero, Allie Clark (r) hold up a copy of their favorite local newspaper, The South Amboy-Sayreville Times. The headline read, "Welcome Back, Jack!" Jack and Allie were at an awards party at Enterprise Fire House.

. McKeon received several awards at a private party at the Enterprise Fire House in South Amboy. Pictured (l-r) Joe Diehm, Jack, Pete Kenny, and South Amboy City Council President, Jim Reick.

Jack proudly shows Sister Esther Hernandez his new rosary beads that were blessed by the Pope.

2004-South Amboy Mayor John T. O'Leary (l) presents Jack McKeon (c) with a beautiful plaque from the City of South Amboy at the Tribute/Dinner. Co-chairman of the event's committee, Mickey Gross (r) proudly looks on.

Jack (c) is reunited with St. Mary's teammate from the 1940's, Leo Kedzierski (l), who played professional baseball. That's Leo's wife Trudy (r).

McKeon gives an inspirational talk to the students at South Amboy Middle/High School in January 2004.

189

*2004-South Amboy Elementary School principal, Carol Galley (l) presented a
Certificate of Appreciation to Jack after he spoke to the entire school.*

*Jack also brought a positive message to the entire student bodies at Cardinal McCarrick High School
and St. Mary Elementary School. Mrs. Cahill, the principal is seated (l).*

Dr. Frank Ianniruberto, principal (r) leads the applause for McKeon after he completed his uplifting talk to the students at Cardinal McCarrick High School.

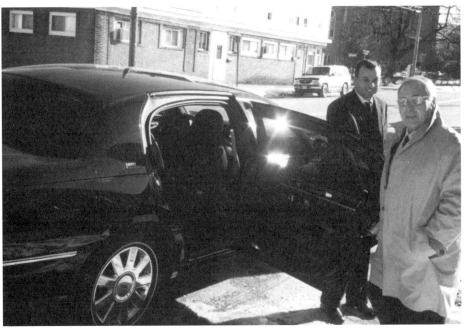

In an exclusive South Amboy-Sayreville Times photo, Jack, after speaking to the school students, is whisked away in a limo that would take him to the airport for his flight to Washington, D.C. to be honored with the Florida Marlins by President George W. Bush at the White House.

191

2004-Pictured in the V.I.P. Room of The Pines in Edison, N.J., prior to the New Jersey Sportswriters Association's 68th Annual Banquet are (l-r) former Yankee great and manager of the Somerset Patriots, Sparky Lyle, Jack McKeon, former Yankee Allie Clark, and South Amboy's Chief of Police, Jim Wallis.

Jack's wife Carol, proudly holds the "Manager of The Year" trophy he received from the New Jersey Sportswriters Association. He was also chosen as their "Man of The Year."

2004-Jack overlooks all the candidates for the Marlins team during Spring Training.

McKeon walks toward the dugout at the Marlins Spring Training site at Jupiter, Florida.

Jim "Kitty" Kaat visited Jack in March 2004 at Spring Training. Kaat, who played for McKeon in the minor leagues, was one of his most successful players.

Fox Sports Network's sportscaster, Craig Minervini (r) interviews Jack (l) on their pre-game show, "Touching All The Bases With Jack McKeon.

Legendary baseball executive, Syd Thrift, scouted for McKeon when he managed the Kansas City Royals.

Jack is shown in his office at Jupiter, Florida during Spring Training 2004. He's holding up a copy of an advertisement he endorsed for Spray Nine.

Jack McKeon (r) gets a lesson in the Korean language from Hee Seop Choi's interpreter during Spring Training.

Jack (l) and author Tom Burkard (r) are pictured at the Reds' Cinergy Field during McKeon's last weekend as manager in September 2000.
(Photo courtsey of Joe Morris)

Talkin' About Pokey, Win #900, Etc. With Jack

On August 30, 2004 in the visiting manager's office at Shea Stadium, Jack and I chatted about an interesting plate of subjects ranging from Pokey Reese to McKeon's 900th big league win, what the rest of the '04 season looked like, and if he was coming back to manage the Florida Marlins in 2005.

Back in your days at Cincinnati, it's been said that you refused to include second baseman Pokey Reese in any packages that would bring Ken Griffey Jr. from the Seattle Mariners to the Reds. Why?

"He was an All-Star and Golden Glove. I thought he was the catalyst in that infield. I certainly didn't want to give up a great defensive player to be thrown in the deal just to get another bat."

How did it feel to win your 900th game in the major leagues?

"I don't even think about numbers. I wouldn't even realize I was close unless someone told me. Now, I have an idea that I'm gonna be reaching 1,000, hopefully if I decide to stay in this thing."

How does it look for the Marlins for the rest of the season?

"We've got a lot of spark, but it's just a question of good pitching and timely hitting. It's a case of getting lucky now. We've got some big roadblocks in front of us. We're in pretty much the same position as we were last season, we might have had a little more time. We were four games out, three at the most this time of the year. We got the Cubs in front of us, and we play them six games. So, we have a chance to decide our own destiny."

Are you coming back to manage the Marlins in 2005?

First of all, it's not my decision. It's a two-way, do they want you back, or do I want to come back? I'm pretty sure they want me back. Do I wanna go back, I don't know. Right now, I'd have to say yes. That's what I told Tim McCarver. I said I'd like to go two more years, so I could become the second oldest manager behind Connie Mack. Right now, I'm third, and I'd like to eke out Casey Stengel. Casey was 75, so I'll need next year and the year after."

Jack Predicts Hall-of-Fame For Current Managers

Marlins' manager, Jack McKeon, in a September 2004 interview at Shea Stadium talked about the Hall-of-Fame, and said that, "With their great records and outstanding credentials, Bobby Cox, Tony LaRussa and Joe Torre should make it to the Hall-of-Fame."

Marlins Won Nine Straight Tied Team Record

In September 2004, the Marlins defeated the New York Mets, 3-0 to capture their ninth consecutive victory, and in doing so, tied the franchise record. It was also the tenth straight win over the New Yorkers. Josh Beckett pitched 8 scoreless innings, and Armando Benitez notched his 41st save. Paul LoDuca blasted a 2-run homer for manager Jack McKeon's club.

Toughin' It During The Hurricane

In Septmeber 2004, Florida was hit hard by Hurricane Frances. As it hammered South Florida, several players, coaches and manager Jack McKeon hunkered down at Pro Player Stadium for three days.

To pass the time, they watched TV, played cards, took a sauna bath, and for dinner they ate spaghetti and meatballs. The group was fortunate, because most of the state lost its power, but not at the ballpark.

Jack slept on a couch during the three-day hiatus, and likened it to a "country club or a resort." He called his wife Carol in North Carolina, and she said that he was a happy guy, because he finally got to sleep at the ballpark.

The Jack & Ozzie Show

The Marlins were forced by the threat of Hurricane Ivan to change their venue to Chicago's U.S. Cellular Field for two "home" games against the Montreal Expos in September 2004.

This provided some good-time fun for Jack and White Sox manager, Ozzie Guillen, who was the Marlins' third base coach on the 2003 World Championship team. McKeon settled into Guillen's manager's office, and joked that he heard Ozzie was worried about him taking his wife's pictures off the wall. Instead, the Marlins' skipper kicked back, and flipped through Ozzie's checkbook, and lit up one of his favorite cigars.

Marlins Set Shutout Record

On September 19, 2004, the Florida Marlins defeated first place Atlanta, 3-0, to set a team record with its 14th shutout of the season, also the most in the big leagues. Ismael Valdez allowed only two hits over six innings, for the big win. Guillermo Mota and Armando Benitez allowed one hit over the last three innings in relief. Benitez notched his 43rd save of the season. Jeff Conine crashed a 2-run homer.

Weathers Wins For Jack

On September 20, 2004, manger Jack McKeon showed a lot of faith in starting David Weathers in a huge game against the Chicago Cubs, another Wild Card contender.

Weathers, who had been used exclusively as a relief pitcher since 1998 made his first start in over six years a big success. He turned in a stellar performance, allowing only two hits and one run in five innings, to chalk up an important 5-2 victory over the explosive Cubs.

Weathers last started in '98 for the Cincinnati Reds, and none other than manager Jack McKeon, who at the time was the skipper of the Reds club.

Phillies Stop Marlins Streak

Florida's mastery over the Philadelphia Phillies was halted on September 21, 2004 at Pro Player Stadium. The Marlins had won 14 consecutive games at home against the Phillies, dating back to April 2, 2003. All good streaks come to an end, as Philadelphia slipped by McKeon's Marlins, 4-2.

Marlins Fall In Final Home Game of 2004

The Marlins dropped a 9-8, 10-inning heartbreaker to the Phillies in their final home game of the 2004 season at Pro Player Stadium on September 23, 2004. Jimmy Rollins blasted a two-out homer off of the usually hard to hit, Armando Benitez.

Manager Jack McKeon tipped his hat to the Florida fans, and told his players to do the same to thank them for their support during the season.

The Marlins' attendance average at home was 22,091, the best since 1998.

Marlins Eliminated From Postseason Play

It took 155 games, almost an entire season, but the Florida Marlins were officially eliminated from playoff contention on September 26, 2004 by the Atlanta Braves, 6-3. The 2003 World Champion team dropped its sixth consecutive game, the longest losing streak since May 2003, and Florida's overall record stood at 79-76.

Final Interview of 2004

My final 2004 interview with Jack McKeon came on September 30th at the Philadelphia Phillies Citizens Bank Park. It was short compared to others, but still interesting. I asked Jack about Ted Turner, and he said, " Ted was a great guy! I was managing Richmond and he was the owner of the club. We have a great relationship. One time, he wanted me to come in and be his assistant, but at the time, I wanted to manage on the field. Eventually, I went to manage the A's, and he saw me and said, 'You're crazy, you know you're going to get fired.' I said, yeah, I know I'm gonna get fired. He said, 'If you get fired, call me. You can always get a job with me,' but I never took him up on it."

We also talked about some GM jobs that were in the works, but never materialized. I asked him about how he almost became GM of the New York Mets. McKeon responded, "Someone in the baseball industry was feeling me out, to see if I would be interested in the GM position with the Mets, and I said, 'yes,' then all of a sudden, they extended Frank Cashen's contract."

Jack continued, "With Baltimore, it was the same situation. They fired Hank Peters, and asked the Padres permission to talk to me. I flew to Baltimore on Columbus Day, October 12th in '87 or '88. I had had a great interview with owner Edward Bennett Williams. He said to me, 'What are you looking for?' At that time, I was making $300,000, so I said, $400,000 for 5 years or $500,000 for 4 years. I met him next week in Hawaii, and he said, 'You're the best guy I interviewed, but I just can't afford to pay you. I still have to pay Hank Peters contract.'

They hired Roland Hemond at $125,000. If I said $300,000 for one year at a time, I probably would have been hired."

Marlins Finish With Second Straight Winning Season

Manager Jack McKeon guided the 2004 Marlins to their second consecutive winning season with a record of 83 wins and 79 losses, .512 pct. This marked the first time in the club's history that they put together back-to-back winning seasons. Florida finished in third place in the National League's East Division, 12 games behind first place Atlanta, and three games behind the second place Philadelphia Phillies.

McKeon Signs For 2005

On October 2, 2004, the Marlins announced that manager Jack McKeon will be back at the helm for the 2005 season. The positive-thinking McKeon has set two more goals for the future: Winning his 1,000th game in the major leagues, and also passing Casey Stengel, as the second oldest manager in baseball history. In order to pass Casey, Jack would have to come back in 2006 as well.

At the end of the 2004 season, McKeon's career won-lost record stood at (928-861), only 72 wins away from the magical 1,000 mark. He also has a fine (158-128) record since he took over the Marlins' helm in 2003, placing him 3rd in all-time victories for a Florida manager, behind Rene Lachemann (221), and John Boles (165). He should pass both in 2005. McKeon's winning percentage (.552) with the Marlins' is easily the best mark for any manager in the club's history.

Another Hall of Fame Induction

Jack was recently selected for another Hall of Fame! On October 23, 2004, he was honored at The Hilton/Hasbrouck Heights/ Meadowlands in New Jersey by being inducted into the Sports Hall of Fame of New Jersey.

The 12th Class of the Sports Hall of Fame of New Jersey also consisted of former racing car driver, Wally Dallenbach Sr.; Roger "Doc" Cramer, who played in the big leagues from 1929-1938; George Martin, who starred for the New York Giants football team, and was captain of the 1986 Super Bowl champions; Seton Hall University's first 1,000 point scorer, Frank "Pep" Saul, who went on to star in the NBA from 1949-1954; Dr. David Sime who ran in the 100 meters in the '60 Olympics; Former Secretary of Treasury and Director of the Federal Energy Administration under President Nixon, William Simon Sr., who also served on the U.S. Olympic Committee for 30 years; Elaine Zayak, who was a World Skating champion; The St. Benedict's Prep baseball teams from 1947-1950, winners of 64 consecutive games.

New York Mets' broadcasters Keith Hernandez (l) and Fran Healy (r) visit with their good friend, Jack McKeon (c) before the start of a New York Mets-Florida Marlins game in 2004.

Guess What They Said About Jack?...

Pete Rose-

(In his book, *My Prison Without Bars*, Pete talks about his son, Pete Jr.'s treatment by the Reds during his brief stint in the major leagues)

"After Pete struck out, McKeon said, "I guess I've seen all I need to see of that Rose kid. Afterward, Petey was sent back to Triple-A and released the following year. It was not my place to get involved and question Jack McKeon or General Manager Jim Bowden, but I believe they were unfair in their treatment of my son."

Jack McKeon-

(Responding to Pete Rose's comments in his book)

"That's Pete. It was a case of where Bowden brought him up, thought it'd put people in the ballpark. He told me, 'Hey give him one at-bat and get him out of there.' "Pete better get his facts straight. Pete doesn't know the facts. We did him a favor. We bring him up, give the kid a chance and put some people in the ballpark, and this is what I get."

Josh Beckett-

(On Jack McKeon)

"He's a fun guy to play for. He has a way of motivating you."

Ivan Rodriguez-

(After winning Game 7 in the NLCS, he gathered the players in a circle in the clubhouse, and invited McKeon in.)

"As a team, we love you and love what you bring to this team. We're going to win the World Series for you."

Dusty Baker-

(On Jack being selected NL Manager of the Year)

"I like Jack. He earned it. He was saying it took him 27 years to win a championship. I'm on number 12 now. Jack is on what? Fifty something? I don't have nothing to be sad about."

Ivan "Pudge" Rodriguez-

(On Jack McKeon)

"This gentleman does a lot of good things for us. He gives us a good example."

The Florida Marlins' Family Talks About Jack McKeon

Jeffrey Loria (Owner of the Florida Marlins Baseball Club)

I was honored to interview Mr. Jeffrey Loria on July 20, 2004 at Shea Stadium, prior to the Marlins vs. Mets game.

"Jack's been great! He's energized the club. He challenges the players. Every time they walk into the clubhouse, he's got something to say to everybody. He needles them when they need to be needled, and he's really got his hand on the pulse of everything in that clubhouse."

When asked to describe last year's fantastic ride to the World Series Championship, he said, "It turned around about a week or 10 days after Jack came on board. Experience does count. When people started criticizing us for hiring a man who is 72 years old, I told everybody then, and I'll say it again, it's not about your age, it's about your experience. Jack had nothing but great experience. From management all the way down to being a player in the minor leagues. He wasn't an entirely great player, but he certainly turned out to be a great manager, and a great human being to be around. Mostly, he's a great human being. He's encouraging and uplifting all the time. He doesn't miss anything, and we wish him nothing but good health."

What highlight stands out most from the great 2003 season for Jeffrey Loria?

"I think the one that stands out the most and summed up the whole season last year, was when he made a decision which went counter to normal practice, or he just felt in his gut that he was going to start Josh Beckett at the end, and the rest is history."

Dan Jennings (Marlins Vice-President of Player Personnel)

Dan Jennings, VP of Player Personnel for the Marlins had plenty to say about McKeon during our interview at Shea Stadium on July 20, 2004.

"Working with Jack is very fun. There's never a dull moment, and he's what I consider a dying breed. He's a baseball guy that has a passion for what he does. He genuinely loves the game, and one thing he said way back, that I thought made more sense than anything was when he delivered the message to the players that he didn't need this job. He's doing this job because there's a passion for it.

Jack's a guy who no matter the good or bad, there's no panic. Especially last year, when most of us for the first time were in a pennant race, and you have decisions to make, and go acquire talent. You've got a guy there who is kind of a calming force through everything we tried to do. He's a good guy to bounce ideas off of. Ultimately, a manager's got to win. He has been on both sides and understands there are financial limitations. There are limitations, prospects you would not want to move, so we've drawn on his experiences as a GM and as a manager, and it was a magical ride. The crowning moment was seeing these kids lift him up and carry him off the field. It just had a storybook ending. The only thing that would have made it better was if he had a cigar right away, and it just would have been a fitting visual image.

I remember his interview, and he said, 'What the hell is age? It's only a number.' It's like my father told me one time when he retired from coaching and teaching, and he got right back in. He said, 'Son, there's only one major event left in my life, and I'm not ready for that yet.'

Jack may be 73, but absolutely doesn't act it. One day last year, he goes out everyday to walk an hour before the game, and he's got on those rubber pants that he walks in, and lights up about an 8-inch stogie, and I said, 'Jack, you're kind of defeating the purpose, aren't you? He said, "Son, at my age, I'm just playing for a tie."

Bill Beck (Florida Marlins Director of Team Travel)

"I first met Jack in December 1968, and then we were in Omaha. He became the manager and the team won the pennant in '69 and '70 in the American Association, and he managed there until '73, when he went to the big leagues.

I ended up being with him in Kansas City for part of '74 and '75. Then he was out as manager, but we always stayed in touch. When he became General Manager in San Diego, he brought me there in January 1984, and I was with him for seven years there. In '84, we won the National League Championship, and went to the World Series. I never thought we'd be together with four organizations, but here he is managing the Marlins, and of course, in 2003, winning the World Series. It was by far, the most special year in the 35 years I've had in baseball.

I've worked with 15 managers, and with Jack, now three times as manager, and he's very patient. He's demanding, but very patient with players. He's grown too. He's gotten better as the years go by. In Jack's case, he's a great judge of players and talent. That is big! The good strategy is that which works. You can question any managers' strategy if it backfires. Jack is by far and away the best I've worked with in judging talent and who can play. He can see a guy play for two or three days, and say this guy's gonna be a good player in two years, or this guy's never gonna be a good player, which is very hard to do. I can't think over the years of him being wrong hardly at all.

Bill tells the following legendary story about Jack:

"We were walking down the street in Oklahoma City one night, Jack, the trainer, and I, and this is in 1969, my first season with him. It's late at night, and a panhandler comes up to him and says, 'Hey buddy, can you give me some money?' Jack grabs the guy by the coat lapel, lifts him in the air, and I'm going, 'whoa,' and Jack says 'Look, I'm working this side of the street. Get over there on the other side.' The guy says okay and scurries across the street."

Steve Copses (Florida Marlins' Director of Media Relations)

As Director of Media Relations with the Marlins, Steve Copses has worked very closely with Jack McKeon since he became manager in 2003. In an interview at Shea Stadium on July 20, 2004, Steve said:

"Jack is tremendous! He's a great guy! He's tough, but fun. He's always here to do whatever we need to do for the team, players and media. He's very media friendly. He's got a lot of stories he likes to tell, and he keeps everybody laughing.

He makes fun of his own age. He's got all that experience. Why do you penalize age?

I really enjoy Jack's version of "The Name Game." He always messes everybody's name up on purpose, and keeps everybody on their feet. It's nice to be around to see the guys come by and they start playing back with his name. That's the fun part of the game. They all realize its for a laugh and keeps everybody loose."

Craig Minervini (Pre-Game Host/In-Game Reporter, Fox Sports Net)

Sportscaster Craig Minervini has known McKeon since he took over the Marlins in May of 2003, and this year has worked closely with him on the air. In an interview at Shea Stadium on July 20, 2004, Minervini had plenty to say about the Marlins' manager.

"I remember our first show was in San Diego, and I didn't know him at all. We do the Marlins Weekly Show and also an everyday pre-game show. I love talking to Jack! We come up with some "Tales of Trader Jack." I learned more about his minor league outfielder Chuck Weatherspoon in stories that we talk about on the show. I actually met him in Houston. I was dying to meet him after hearing all of Jack's funny stories about him. Some people don't realize that Jack has a heck of a sense of humor, and it comes out in a unique way. I like to come up with light, funny topics. We talk more than baseball, but it's a joy to talk to him about it. He obviously has got a wealth of information. His philosophies are sometimes different than mine and others, and yet how many times I've seen it and go whoa! Then all of a sudden it worked. He's been great to work with. The show is going good.

Every show is called "Touching All The Bases With Jack McKeon." It's in every pre-game show, a segment of 3-4 minutes, and we kick around last night's game. Sometimes, we just talk about whatever is going on. Today, we talked about his days at Seton Hall. We also talk about some of his minor league stories or major league. Funny things that come up along the way. A lot of times, we'll talk about a key decision, whether it was positive or negative. Sometimes, a decision doesn't work. To me, that's the fun of baseball. It's not always fun for the manager, but to look at the decision and second guess it, agree with it or not, it's fun for the fans to kick around. He's very receptive to that. He can't go up and hit for the players. He's made the moves. That's all you can do in his job is make the moves, and sometimes they don't work. This year, they haven't worked, only because they haven't been executed. They haven't executed well.

It's been a lot of fun working with him. I think he enjoys it too. He reminds me of my dad, a lot too, and I know my dad enjoyed meeting him in Chicago last year. They talked about old New York baseball days. I like to pick Jack's mind a little bit. He'll come over and give me tips. Like for example, last year at All-Star break, right before I went on, he came over and said, 'How much time you got?' I said a minute, and he said, 'I got some news.' I got a cue in my ear, 45 seconds. I said, Good news? He puts his thumb up. 30 seconds. What is it? 'Urbina.' You gonna get him, you got him? 'Yeah.' 15 seconds. Done deal? 'Yeah. Are you still on the air?' Yeah. So, I had Urbina right off the bat. He's aware of what we (The media) do. He's very media savvy, and it's nice to work with a manager who understands his own role, and also likes talking to the press, and getting the word out. He's a great ambassador."

The Florida Marlins Coaches

The Florida Marlins coaches shared their views and stories about manager Jack McKeon. The following are from individual interviews conducted from March 19-26 at Spring Training 2004 in Jupiter, Florida:

Jeff Cox (Third Base Coach)

"Jack is unbelievable! Honestly, he reminds me of my father. My father's a brilliant man. He was a Lieutenant Colonel in the U.S. Air Force. He's a college professor emeritus. Jack is brilliant baseball wise. He knows how to get along with people, and get the best out of them. He manages with iron fists and velvet gloves. It's just a pleasure in my life. Having played at the Kansas City Royals Baseball Academy when I was 17 years old, and sitting on the grass and have major league manager, Jack McKeon of the Kansas City Royals come down and speak to us about playing winning baseball. My goodness, 30 years later, I'm one of his coaches!

He's very unique in his own way of managing. He's just a wealth of knowledge and nothing gets by him. It's a wonder to be around him everyday, and kind of appreciate the dedication and all he's put through in his life to learn this game, to get along with people, let alone fans and media. He's as unique as you'll ever find a baseball man, let alone a person."

Wayne Rosenthal (Pitching Coach)
"It was interesting the first couple weeks when Jack became manager, but once we got to rhythm, talking to him and everything, it was easy working with him. He would always explain stuff to me and helped me better understand what needs to be done. He's a very smart man, knows what he's doing, has strong opinions. He asks your opinion too. He wants to know what you think, but he makes the decision. He's helped me out a lot. This year in Spring Training, we're a lot more comfortable around each other. It's been a pleasure working with him.

He's an old-school type guy, strong-willed, and knows what he wants. He knows what to get out of the players. I played for one guy in the big leagues, Bobby Valentine. With Jack, it's a love/hate relationship for the players. He gets on them when he needs to, and they respect that. He's with them and jokes around when he needs to. That's kind of the way it should be. Sometimes, you're gonna love him, and sometimes you're gonna hate him, and he doesn't care what people think about him. He's gonna say his piece, and say what he wants. I respect him for that. He says it to me too. The only way you're gonna learn is to hear the truth, and he tells you the truth."

Bill Robinson (Hitting Coach)
"Jack is very loosey-goosey. He doesn't take anything real serious. It's not a life or death situation. He's the kind of guy that believes in it's a marathon race, it's not a sprint. So, he doesn't take a win or loss very serious. It's a long, grueling season, so he's on an even keel. He's a winner. The man is known for turning ballclubs around. He certainly came here, and the seed was planted by other people, and Jack came in and solidified the whole thing. He's a no-nonsense guy. You're gonna do it his way. I think players in general want the discipline, and Jack is certainly old-school and will give the discipline that players need.

Perry Hill (First Base Coach)
"Number one, he's one of the best baseball men I've ever been around. Number two, he lets his coaches coach, and number three, there's never a dull moment. He keeps his sense of humor and very highly competitive and serious business. He keeps a light-hearted approach and has a sense of humor. He's a real easy guy to work for.

Doug Davis (Bench Coach)

"I think from my standpoint, being a young coach and somebody who hasn't spent a lot of time in the major leagues, it's just a tremendous experience being with somebody who's been in the game as long as he has. I know he's got about as much experience to draw from. I think for me it's just a matter of being around him and trying to pay attention to what he does in making the decisions he makes, and why he makes them. I think he has a great feel for the game. I've managed too, in the past, but again not at this level. I haven't dealt with players at this level. For me, its just the experience of being around him, watching him make decisions and why he's doing the things that he does. How he treats players, how he handles players. How he handles situations and also how he handles fans and media.

You have to put Jack right at the top from the standpoint if you're a player. He's certainly a player's manager, but he lets everybody know where they stand and what he expects from them. There's never any questions when it comes to Jack. You know exactly what he wants you to do, and if you're doing something good, he lets you know, and if you're doing something he'd like to see change, he lets you know that too. I think he's very straight-forward and honest in that sense, and that's a very good attribute for a manager to have. The managers I've been around, all have pluses and minuses. There aren't many negatives with Jack. For the most part, it's all positive. He just makes you feel very good about being here, and being a part of this."

Tony Taylor (Bullpen Coach)

"He's old-time (old-school). It's great working with him. He's a fine man, and number one, he's a good baseball man. He knows the game. He's done a tremendous job for the Marlins for two years he's been here. Anytime you have a good baseball man on the team, they do a good job. He's a great and tremendous man to work for. He's very patient, very honest and the ballplayers like him, and he treats them the way you're supposed to. Everybody loves him!"

Tony Perez (Special Assistant To The President; Major League Baseball Hall-of-Famer)

"It's great working with Jack. Jack is an oldtimer. I knew him since he was in San Diego. We've run into each other almost every year since I've been in baseball. He's nice, he knows the game, and we talk a lot. It's nice to be with him and work with him. He knows almost everybody, all the players. He don't have to be with the players for 20 years, but he knows them. He watches them play and is around them in Spring Training.

He does a good job with everybody. He uses everybody on the team, all 25 guys. He wants to win the game and is not afraid to use anybody."

Pierre Arsenault (Bullpen Coordinator)

"Wow! I've been doing this for 18 years and it's the first time I reached the playoffs, and I never imagined being in a World Series game, and Jack comes in and not only do we get to the playoffs, but we win the World Series. He was just a breath of fresh air for everybody. He just came in and had a job to do, and he did it well. It's great to work for him because he has high expectations of everybody, and wants everybody to do their work, but at the same time, he's very positive and communicates with everybody, which is nice. You've got some managers you don't even see that much and hear from, but with him, he's always talking and you always feel like you're part of the action, or you're trying to help out. The first manager I worked for was Buck Rodgers, which kind of reminds me of Jack in the sense that Buck was loosey-goosey when he was off the field, but when he was on the field, he had expectations.

I just think Jack stacks up with the best that I've been able to work with. Also, because of the way he treated me and my family. I think that's important. He always talks about his family and wants a family atmosphere, and that's what he brings. Some guys talk about it, but they don't bring it to the table. He actually backed up all his actions, and took care of everybody, and he was great! He's a great manager to work for!

I think everybody at first was shocked to hear that he was coming back, because he had been out of the game, so you don't know what to expect. You hear that he's an old-time guy, but he relates well with all the young players, and he's not afraid to kick them in the butt when they had to be kicked in the butt, which is refreshing in today's game. I think today, a lot of managers are scared to kick them in the butt, because they make more money than the manager does. That was probably the turning point for us, that he wasn't afraid to kick some butts and get into some people's faces, and tell them the truth, as opposed to telling them what they wanted to hear."

Florida Marlins' Players Talk About Jack

Juan Pierre (Marlins' outstanding center fielder)

In an interview on June 5, 2004 in the visitors clubhouse at Shea Stadium, the Marlins' talented 2003 Stolen Base Champion spoke in great detail about manager Jack McKeon.

I asked the Marlins' outstanding center fielder what it was like to play for Jack McKeon, and he responded:

"It's almost like playing for your grandfather. He gets on you when you're doing stuff wrong, but he always loves you and pulls for you. He's very stern. He knows what he wants and knows what you can do, and he wants you to go out there and do it. He knows sometimes it's not going to happen. He's just great because he lets you go out there and play. He more or less lets you figure it out yourself. He doesn't have to tell you everything. He makes you almost be held accountable for everything on the field. Last year, we grew as a team, and this year continuing, where a lot of young guys are learning how to play. They're pretty much on their own, but he steps in every now and then if he sees something, but for the most part, he just lets you go out there and play.

Last year was a really exciting run. We were just trying to get to .500 and make it respectable, and see what happens after that. We got to .500 and continued to play well. He was really energetic and everybody was talking about how old he was. He would get to the yard, walk three miles while smoking cigars. He was himself. You couldn't help but get energized when you saw him at seventy-some years old, walking and stuff. There was no trying to come in here tired. There's no room for that."

How does Jack McKeon stack up against other managers you played for?

"He's up there at the top because for the most part, he just lets me go out there and play. When I was a rookie, managers had a tighter grip on me, but he just says go out and play, be yourself. To win the World Series with him is always going to be a special place with me. He definitely has helped me out a lot. Just by all the things he would tell me to look for and things like that. It's awesome having him as a manager."

Dontrelle Willis-(2003 National League Rookie-of-The-Year)

The Marlins talented left-handed pitcher, Dontrelle Willis had some wonderful things to say about skipper Jack McKeon in an August 31, 2003 interview at Shea Stadium.

I asked him what it was like to play for manager Jack McKeon, and he said:

"It's baseball man. He just wants us to go out there and work hard. That's all he asks. Just go out there and put our all into it everyday. Just go there and try to better yourself.

I've been fortunate to play with managers that just want you to go out there, work hard, and play the game of baseball. I've been real lucky. It's all the same. Go out there and pitch your heart out and believe in everything you work for. Especially if you go out there when you're struggling and you believe in everything you're doing, and you believe in your processing, he won't get upset at you.

He's very knowledgeable. He's been around some teams, and had some good players, so he definitely has had some success. You have to take that into consideration.

Last year, it was definitely fun. It helped us to realize that all it takes is 25 guys believing in each other, and anything could be possible. It was fun to play at Yankee Stadium. There were a lot of historical events going on there. It was fun to beat them at their own stadium. A lot of people haven't accomplished that."

Mike Mordecai (Utility Player)

In an interview at Shea Stadium on August 31, 2003, Mike Mordecai talked about playing for Jack McKeon:

"It's very easy playing for Jack. Just come out and play baseball, that's it. He doesn't ask very much of you, just to play hard and smart baseball. Every manager I've ever played for has been really good to play for. Bobby Cox, Felipe Alou, Jeff Torborg, Frank Robinson and Jack. They're all very similar in that they expect you to show up and play hard, that's it. Basically, that's all they ever ask.

Jack, I think, has been around long enough and realizes how he can help guys out on various parts of their game. One of the main big things Jack stresses is that there are no egos here. We're here to win ballgames. 'I don't care which guy, one through 25, you're all here to help us win ballgames. Check your ego at the door.' That's it. That's huge!

I was extremely happy for Jack to win the World Series because he's been in the game as long as he has, and he finally got to experience all that which is great. I was fortunate enough to play in Atlanta my first three years, and I was in the playoffs every year, and two World Series my first two years, and we won it my very first year. You see a guy like Jack who's been in the game forever, and never got to experience that. I was extremely happy for him, and I know he enjoyed every bit of it. Being the type of manager he is, he says 'I couldn't do it without my players,' so he realizes that the players are the ticket, and he lets the players play, but play hard and play smart."

Josh Willingham

Florida's rookie catcher, Josh Willingham was up with the big club for about a week when I caught up with him in the visitors dugout at Shea Stadium before the Marlins took on the Mets on July 19, 2004. I asked him what it was like to play for manager Jack McKeon. He responded:

It's been great! He's been great to me, and made me feel comfortable, as soon as I came into the clubhouse my first day. It was just, 'Hey how you doin'? This is just another game, go get 'em!' So, I felt comfortable as soon as I walked in the dugout. It's been a great experience!"

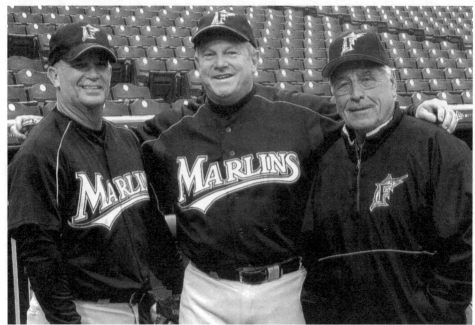

2004-Manager Jack McKeon (r) poses with first base coach Perry Hill (l) and third base coach Jeff Cox (c)

Jack's Former Players, Coach Share Their Memories

Fran Healy

Fran Healy, a talented Sportscaster for the Mets' Fox Sports New York/MSG cable casting team, has known Jack McKeon for many years, and remained good friends. He was the starting catcher for McKeon's first major league club, the 1973 Kansas City Royals, and also played under Jack's managerial genius in 1974-75.

I caught up with the very busy Healy for this interview at Shea Stadium on June 4, 2004 prior to the Marlins-Mets game. Fran shared many happy memories and humorous stories about his former manager.

"I met Jack McKeon in 1969. I played in a minor league game in Spring Training, and I was with the major league team, and we were in Miami, Florida. I was playing and I got a base hit, and I'm on first base, late in the game, and he pinch-ran for me. That's the only time in my whole career anybody pinch-ran for me. I went in the dugout and said, 'What the hell are you thinking about?' Jack said, 'What do you mean?' I said, 'I can run. I know you were a catcher and couldn't run, but give me a shot at it.' I ended up stealing 16 bases for him in the big leagues. That was my introduction to Jack. He was one of the greatest characters I've ever met.

212

He comes up to my waist, and he used to drive me nuts in the minor leagues. I played in 1969 and 1970, and he used to always lecture me. He lectured me one day, and it was the funniest thing. I'm in the outfield, standing there, and I had my back to him. I had a bad back, and to brace it, I would fold my arms. So, he thought the body language was not too good. So, he jumped all over me about the body language, and I had my arms folded. I said I got a bad back, and he said, 'I don't believe it,' and walked away. He's been like that ever since I've known him.

He's been by far the best manager I've ever played with. He's as good as any manager I've ever seen. If they (The Marlins) win this year, he belongs in the Hall-of-Fame. He should have been "Manager of the Year" in 1973, when I played for him with the Royals. He took an expansion team that wasn't doing anything. When he took it over, he built that team and it was ready to win. Herzog took it over and they won it, and Herzog said, 'This team was ready to win.' It was ready to win because Jack's decisions about talent, and who to put on the field. But, he to me is a baseball genius."

One time when I was playing for him, we were in Texas. When you're on the field, you're concerned about getting your hits and winning the ballgame. I'm catching and there's a ball hit down the right field line at the old Texas Stadium. The sun came over the right field fence, and I think the umpire, who I believe was Bill Deegan, lost the ball in the sun. When he turned to look and spot the ball, it was 30 feet foul. This was a no brainer. Luckily, he calls it fair ball, because he clearly lost it. Jack comes out of the dugout, you know, he's like that bobblehead Jack, and he's jawing with him. He gets thrown out of the game, so he calmly walks down to first base, where I'm standing behind home plate and says, 'Listen, next time something like that happens, I want you to faint and we're going to come out with a stretcher and carry you off the field.' I said, 'That's not happening. I gotta hit. These guys will kill me.' But, he's a character.

Another time, in Triple-A ball, we had a young pitcher, I think his name was Montgomery, and he was getting hit pretty hard, so Jack went out to remove him from the game. We had a guy named Jones in bullpen. Now he's a veteran on his way out. So, we're standing on the mound, Jack called him in, and as he's making his way to the mound, Montgomery had a lot of excuses as to what happened. He continued to talk and I'm thinking this is not a good scene. As Jonesy comes towards the mound, he's on the outfield grass, you know you usually walk straight in from left field. Jack says to him, 'Hey Jonesy, go over by the dugout and come that way to the mound. Even I'm looking at him, 'What the hell is he doing?' So, Jonesy comes around and goes out to the mound. Now Jonesy was this very conservative, quiet accountant in the off-season. He gets to the mound and said, 'Jack, what'd you want me to walk like that for?'

Jack said, ' Well, because he just threw so much crap, you would step in it.'

This is not a smooth relationship. This was a rough relationship. I mean I treasure it. He would stay on me, stay on me. He told me a story how he stays on Josh Beckett, and I told Beckett, 'You know what the problem is? He doesn't like anybody over 6 foot 3.'

I can remember riding in buses in Triple-A ball, and I have trouble sleeping, even to this day. Well, Jack of course wants to talk to everybody. So everybody's asleep, so I'd go up and I'd sit with him. He'd have a cigar going on the bus. He'd be telling me New Jersey stories about the taxi cab company. I was in stitches. He was the one thing that kept me going, because when you're not sleeping, it's tough. I used to sit and listen to him tell those great stories. I loved those stories!

In Triple-A ball, I played with his team. I would say everybody on the team would probably say its the greatest team ever assembled. We had the right manager, because he knew exactly what to do. If you worked hard on the field, you could do things off the field that most managers would frown upon. Not him! He wouldn't care. When you were on the field, he would drive you nuts. Most things that would alarm other managers, wouldn't alarm him.

There was a guy from New Jersey, Dick Estelle, a good pitcher, who hurt his arm. He was pitching against us, he's a lefty, I'm a righty hitter. We have a lot of right-handed hitters in the lineup, and we're facing a sore-armed pitcher. He had great stuff when he was healthy, but this night, he had a sore arm, and early in the game, Jack goes out to argue a pitch. We're in the dugout, and Estelle is on the mound. We're waiting for Jack to get done. All of a sudden, Estelle gets upset with Jack's arguing. He says something, and Jack says something. They get in a fight, and they both get thrown out of the game. So we got a sore-armed pitcher getting thrown out of the game, because Jack was in a fight with him in the first inning. The stories of Jack are just incredible! Smoking that cigar!

He was listening to me one day in Kansas City. Harmon Killebrew was in the car, and Jack was driving. I was giving directions. On purpose, I was giving him wrong directions. Harmon was watching the road closely, and Jack's smoking his cigar and driving. "Killer" knows we're going the wrong way. Finally, after about 15 minutes, he said, 'Jack, don't listen to him. He's doing this on purpose.'

I treasure our relationship and I'm very happy for the success of the Marlins, because at times, he ended up leaving certain areas because of players not being able to adjust to his discipline or his mindset as an old-timer. I still see him say to young pitchers, 'Don't throw today on the side. Throw in the bullpen, because I might want you to get a hitter out.' Well, you know that's a cardinal sin today. You can't do that, but he still does it. I love it!

Frank White

Jack McKeon was very impressed with young and talented second baseman, Frank White in 1973, so high on the youngster's ability that he battled the front office to bring him up from the minor leagues when shortstop Freddy Patek was injured.

McKeon, one of baseball's greatest judges of player potential won, and the rest is history! White went on to an outstanding career, finishing with over 2,000 hits, eight Golden Glove Awards, many All-Star selections, and was elected to the Kansas City Royals' Hall-of-Fame. He is the greatest second sacker in Royals' history.

In 2004, Frank managed the Royals' Wichita farm club, and spoke kindly of his days as a player under Jack McKeon:

"I remember when I was in AAA and Jack wanted me to come up when Freddy Patek got hurt, and the front office said 'no.' Jack said that if he couldn't have me, then he didn't want anyone. That's how I got to the big leagues.

Playing for Jack was great, because he was so great with young players. He let us play, and he is a good motivator.

Frank said that, "I wasn't surprised when Jack returned to baseball and won the World Series because he can motivate young players, and he's always positive. He can make you play up to and beyond your potential."

Goose Gossage

In 1984, his first season with the San Diego Padres, Rich "Goose" Gossage helped lead the club to its first National League pennant by notching 25 saves and 10 victories. "Trader Jack" McKeon was the General Manager of the Padres, and Gossage commented on the colorful GM:

"Jack was very easy-going, and it was a real pleasure to play for him. My greatest memory of Jack was watching him win the World Series. I was so happy for him. Especially at his age. What a great story!

Paul Schaal

Paul Schaal was a fine major league third baseman, who started and batted a fine .288 for Jack McKeon's first big league ball club, the 1973 Kansas City Royals. He had great things to say about McKeon:

"I enjoyed my time playing for Jack. With Jack, we always knew where he stood, what our role on the team was, and what was expected of us. He never put undo pressure on a player. His philosophy was to have fun playing this great game. Give your best and winning will take care of itself.

Jack was a player's manager, not a front office manager. He had a great sense of humor. He could take jokes and kidding from players, as well as dish it out himself. Winning baseball is a trickle-down situation. Good attitudes are contagious, and Jack was a great leader!"

When asked if he was surprised that Jack came back to baseball at age 72 and won the World Series, he responded, "No. Jack belongs on the field with the players. To reach the major leagues as a player, the talent must be there. To mold that talent and to bring out the best in both confidence and ability from the players is the role of a great manager. Jack had/has that talent."

Red Schoendienst

Major League Baseball Hall of Famer, Red Schoendienst coached for Jack McKeon in 1977, when he managed the Oakland A's. In an interview with Red during Spring Training 2004, he said the following about McKeon:

"I coached for Jack at Oakland. Jack's a good baseball man and he knows baseball. He more or less was everything when he was there with Charlie Finley. I said to Jack, 'You'd be an outstanding GM. You're an outstanding manager. You know baseball.'

He knows how to handle ballplayers. I was really pulling for him last year, and I was glad to see him win. He had young ballplayers, and a guy like that really knows his baseball. I'm really glad he won last year!"

Paul Splittorff

The ace of McKeon's Kansas City Royals '73 squad with a (20-11) record, lefty Paul Splittorff was one of Jack's favorite players of all-time. When asked what it was like to play for McKeon, he said:

"He was great! His interest was the young players, and I was at that time. He gave me an opportunity in 1969, and pushed for me in 1971."

Splittorff said that his greatest memory of Jack was that "He kept it light and fun."

Was he surprised that Jack came back to baseball at age 72 and won the World Series?

"I guess it's always a surprise when a guy is out of the game completely, and then gets back in-especially at that age. It was a perfect team and time for him."

Mike Cameron

Mike Cameron, a talented, power-hitting center fielder played for Jack McKeon on the Cincinnati Reds. In an interview at Shea Stadium on July 19, 2004, Cameron, now playing for the New York Mets commented on his former skipper:

"He's a good man. He gave me the opportunity at such a young age to go out and play everyday. He's a guy that really sticks up for you. He's been around baseball for about a million years, so he knows the ins and outs of the game.

He's seen a lot of great players come and go. For me, to be able to share some of the experiences myself that he's went through is definitely a big help.

I'm very happy for him for things that have happened more recently, because the way it happened when he left Cincinnati in 2000, wasn't supposed to happen. We all know how the game is, it's part of a business. For him to get the opportunity to come back and win a World Series, and lead a young team like the Marlins is a special thing for him.

If I have one thing to say about the man, it's a blessing to have someone on your side like that . He's probably over there (In the visitors dugout) smoking a cigar right now, joked Cameron. (Mike was exactly right about that).

He's a good dude. He stuck me in the lineup every single day. He's a good motivator. A lot of people don't know about it. Everyone has a different type of motivation, but his was hands on. He let you know right in your face what was going on, some of the reasons why you don't play well or you do play well. I've had two managers like that, he was one of them, and the other was Lou Piniella. Jack's a good dude!

Jack McKeon Talks About Mike Cameron

The following day, July 20, 2004 at Shea Stadium, I asked Jack about Mike Cameron, and he said:

"He's a good player. There's no question about it. He probably had his best years for me over in Cincinnati. He got his first real chance to play as a regular with me. He'll hit 20 home runs for the Mets, play outstanding defense, and he'll steal a lot of bases. He's a good ballplayer, a team player, and he enjoys playing the game."

Jim "Kitty" Kaat

Current New York Yankees' sportscaster, Jim "Kitty" Kaat , in his first year of pro ball, played for manager Jack McKeon. Kaat went on to a nearly Hall-of-Fame career with 283 victories and 2,461 strikeouts. He won 20 games three times, and also captured an unbelievable 14 Golden Glove Awards.

I had the opportunity to meet Jim in Spring Training, on March 22, 2004 at Roger Dean Stadium, Jupiter, Florida. He had plenty of praise for his first professional manager.

He said that McKeon's greatest help to his game was "his encouragement." Jack had faith in the young hurler, even when the lefty had a rough start.

Kaat recalled, "I'm like 1-4 and getting hammered, and thinking, 'where can I go from here? I'm in Class C ball. Jack called me and said, 'Jim, you're going to pitch every four days. The organization likes you. You're going to be one of their pitchers. You just relax.' "That turned my year around. Having Jack that year was very important to me," said Kaat.

Jack And The Great Jim Kaat Story

Jack McKeon was 18-year old Jim Kaat's first manager in professional baseball at Missoula, Montana in 1958. He knew that Kaat was very talented and would definitely make the major leagues. Chuck Dressen and Joe Haines, a pitching guru came to watch Kaat pitch, and he won 3-0 on a 3-hitter, as McKeon belted two homers. Afterwards, McKeon asked Haines what he thought about "Kitty" Kaat, and he said, 'pretty good, but he'll never make the bigs.' Jack, who was certain he had a "blue-chipper" in Kaat, bet Haines a steak dinner that Kaat would make the majors within two years. His prediction came true only six months later, when Kaat was called to the parent Washington Senators club.

McKeon said that "If you're scouting with a gun, you don't think he can pitch, but when you're out there and watch him day in and day out, he could put the ball on the black, change speeds, and he can field just as good.

"They laughed at me. 25 years later he was still in the majors and won nearly 300 games (283), and 14 Golden Gloves, which I think tied Brooks Robinson for the most. He was probably the most intelligent pitcher at 18 years old that I've ever been around. He could tell you how to pitch to every hitter in that league.

Calvin Griffith and the Washington Senators took him to the big leagues from Chattanooga after six months in the minors, and he was there (in the majors) for 25 years. He was called up on July 2, 1959, and so was my shortstop at Appleton, Wisconsin, Zoilo Versalles, who later became the American League's MVP."

Dick Schultz

Dick Schultz, a fine pitcher, who played for Jack McKeon in the 1950's, when he managed at Fayetteville, and also Missoula, Montana in the minor leagues, took time out during Spring Training 2004 at the Marlins' Roger Dean Stadium in Jupiter Florida, to share some of his great memories of McKeon.

Dick said, "Playing for Jack McKeon was nothing but fun! We had a great time and learned a lot about baseball. Jack was the kind of guy that you gotta have fun with if you're gonna play the game, or else, he don't need you. We had a lot of fun, but we all worked hard. He had us training very hard. Morning workouts at 8 o'clock, chasing fungoes.

I rate him very high as a manager. I don't think there's anybody I played for is any better. I played for about 10 managers, and I think Jack was the best by far. He was very knowledgeable as a manager. He was a catcher, and he caught me 75% of the time. He was a player/manager. In Fayetteville, he was our catcher, and our manager got fired, and Jack was hired as manager in '55.

That was his first year as manager in pro baseball. He did a great job! We had a good ballclub. We had about 8 major leaguers on the team. Harry Helner, a left-handed pitcher, Curt Howton, left fielder, Jimmy Foxworth, Bucky Jacobs, Ken Deal, a knuckleball pitcher with the Red Sox. I was a 19-year old kid, and for me it was a learning bed to learn to play the game to win, and that's the only way to play it.

I was ecstatic and said, Jack you're on top of the world, when he won the World Series. I kept in touch with Jack over the years, but today is the first time I saw him in over 40 years. He hasn't changed a bit. He's still the same guy I knew as a kid.

I learned to pitch with Jack McKeon, because he taught me how to go in and out, inside, outside, move the ball around, up and down, never in the same place twice, because you get hurt when you do that. Professionals will hurt you if you throw the same pitch in the same spot.

In 1958, I talked Jim Kaat into going to play for Jack at Missoula, Montana instead of going to Chattanooga, where he had a contract. I felt that Jack was the best person in the system to help pitchers, and it worked out. The next year, Kaat went to the big leagues and played for 23 years.

Jack McKeon is a wonderful man to play for in baseball, wherever it may be!"

Syd Thrift Talks About Jack

Longtime, major league baseball executive, Syd Thrift recently spoke about his association with Jack McKeon. We got together in Spring Training 2004 at the Media Dining Room at Roger Dean Stadium in Jupiter, Florida.

"Jack was managing High Point-Thomasville for Kansas City in 1968. Then, Mr. Kauffman and I started the Baseball Academy, and he asked me if I had the pick of all the minor league baseball managers, who would I take. I said, Jack McKeon, and he said, 'who's he?' I said he was a good manager, trust me. Mr. Kauffman got to know Jack at the Academy, and then Jack went to Omaha in Triple A. That's how Jack evolved. I was Director of the Academy. We've known each other a very long time. I was his Advance Scout when he became a major league manager with Kansas City.

He wouldn't let George Brett come to the big leagues until I approved it. It's in the book. He said he wouldn't believe anyone but me, so they sent me to Omaha to look at Brett.

Jack is street-smart. He knows people. He knows how to get the most out of a player. He knows how to lead and manage people. He's managed a long time, and he's learned by doing. He's smart. He's become a better manager every year he's ever managed."

Matt Loughlin-Fox Sports New York Broadcaster Talks About Jack McKeon

Award-winning broadcaster, Matt Loughlin and Jack McKeon both graduated from St. Mary's High School, South Amboy, New Jersey. McKeon was in the class of 1948, and Loughlin graduated in 1975. Through the years, Matt has interviewed Jack many times and has gotten to know him very well. Loughlin gave his personal insights on McKeon on May 6, 2004 at Shea Stadium.

"I've always found Jack to be among the most engaging men in baseball. He's a guy who keeps everything in perspective. Clearly he wants to win. That's what he's paid to do. I remember years ago when I was on ESPN, and started to interview managers during the game. When he was with Cincinnati, he said to me, 'Why don't you come down and talk to me during the game. Come on down and whisper by the corner of the dugout and you'll do an interview with me in the sixth inning.' I said, well, yes. Of course, I was petrified to do it because it's against Major League Baseball rules, but he's thinking ahead. He's a very modern thinker in that way. He's not caught up in convention and things like that.

So, I've always found him to be a fresh breath of air blowing through the game that thinks too much inside the lines, he thinks outside the lines. He's always treated me well. I think he treats everybody well. Not that it really mattered, but he's a little more nicer, a little more welcome and opened, when he found out we shared a background.

The 2003 season for Jack was magical from every perspective. He takes over a team that's well-below .500, in turmoil, not doing everything, and patiently sets the table, sets the tone for them, and they follow. It was wonderful to watch, to see this man who's done so much for baseball in the game, reach the apex with such a young team. There were so many doubters, a franchise faltering with so many issues, and he comes along and just leads them to the World Series.

I like the way he approached it. He spent about a week just watching them, didn't say anything, filled out the lineup card, let them go about their business, and how they prepared, have them play and whatever they did. Then he had a team meeting and basically said, 'You guys don't know what it takes to win. Your preparation is not good. Here's how we're going to do it. If anyone wants to follow, get behind. I'm leading. Anybody else, we'll figure out a way to make you happy elsewhere. That's what they needed. They needed some guidance. He has the right mix of toughness when need be, understanding when it's called for. He was the perfect guy for a team that needed that touch. Obviously, the talent was there."

Publisher Ron Kukulski Remembers Jack

Ron Kukulski (Publisher of Florida New Homes Guide, a Sun-Sentinel Company publication) was the former sports editor of *The News Tribune* in New Jersey, and also lived in South Amboy, McKeon's hometown. He got to know and appreciate Jack through the years. He said:

"I do remember Jack's brother, "Biff" calling me one night at *The News Tribune* offices with the news prior to it breaking, that Jack would be managing this expansion ball club. "Biff" was as proud as can be that his brother would be managing in the majors after paying his dues in the minors. "Biff" gave me all the info about this new expansion team, how Jack was getting this wonderful opportunity, and how he was so proud of his brother, then and not known to "Biff" at the time, for what Jack would go on to accomplish.

My favorite Jack story is how he would go out and "argue" with the umpire to get the crowd fired up. Although his arms were flailing and he was gesturing and waving his hat up and down, he was actually complimenting the umpire on the call. Jack knew then how to play up to the crowd, and he's using that same personality to charm South Florida and inspire the Florida Marlins.

Another tidbit: I sent to Jack a note that "Yash" Lagoda was suffering from cancer and listed "Yash's" home phone number. Jack called "Yash" from the dugout while the Marlins were taking playoff batting practice, and talked with him for about 10 minutes. Those moments were so treasured by "Yash." He told everyone in his neighborhood and had all his neighbors watching every Marlin game as they marched to the World Series Championship. That phone call to "Yash" gained in my heart a very warm spot for Jack, who is never too busy to talk with the fans. In fact, during one afternoon leading up to a playoff game, the Marlins were having computer problems in the ticket sales area. Jack found out about it, went outside and began talking with the fans who were waiting in line. He spent well over an hour talking with fans and signing autographs. Jack has this rare ability to connect with people, which helps make him so successful.

And perhaps a common denominator Jack and I share is we both spent time in Missoula, Montana. I was there in the late '90's for a seminar.

Bill McKeon's Memories
Of His Brother Jack

Jack's younger brother, Bill, nicknamed "Biff" McKeon was a talented catcher, who played in the Braves' farm system. In a May, 2004 interview, he was kind enough to share his lifetime of memories about Jack.

"Jack was a leader from the very beginning of our childhood, as we organized games of sports or fun games of "Steal The City" or "Chase" within the neighborhood of John Street, in South Amboy, New Jersey.

At the tender age of four, on November 11, 1936, Armistice Day, I was engulfed as a human ball of fire, when my winter clothing caught fire at my grandmother and grandfather McKeon's backyard, and whereby being scared and on fire, I ran home. As the fire was blazing from my clothing, big brother John (Jack), who was only five, and turned six within a couple of weeks on November 23rd, tried and tried to tackle me and roll me over to extinguish the flames and fire from my body. Jack showed leadership, responsibility and compassion at this young age of six.

Jack talked my father into starting the famous McKeon Boys Club, where the O'Brien Twins, Jackie and Eddie played along with many other young men who called South Amboy their home. Jack was the team captain and leader, and helped the McKeon's Boys Club win their first championship in the South Amboy Recreational League, where we received red and gold reversible jackets as winners. Jack also scheduled all our games, both home at Veterans or Tigers Field as it was called back then, and is now known as Veterans Memorial Park Home of Jack McKeon Field. We had to battle the Maxfield gang of ballplayers back then, as they considered Tigers Field their property. The Kenny brothers, who also were good baseball players were the leaders.

Chet Meinzer was our coach per say, as we needed an adult, and Walt Mick was our bus driver, as my father purchased a mini van bus for us to travel.

We also had a basketball team, whereby my father purchased a vacant warehouse on Leffert and Feltus Streets for us to practice indoors during the winter months. If not for Jack's love of sports, we wouldn't have had any of these things my father was able to provide.

At the tender age of 16-plus, Jack was asked to organize and coach a bunch of former and present high school players to play in the strong South Amboy City Senior Baseball League. That's where teams like Abby's, Brennan's Nebus', and Nelson's were the cream of South Amboy's baseball talent and competed. South Amboy was loaded with former professional and college baseball players, who knew how to play baseball, and helped the younger players learn the ins and outs of the game. Joe Jerome's Tavern (Now Lagoda's) on Broadway was our sponsor. He treated us to ice cream soda's after every game at Jack's Soda Shop on Stevens Avenue. Most or nearly everyone of us were under 21 years of age. I believe I was the youngest player in the league at 14 years of age. One time, Steve Zebro hit me a grounder at third base, and Jack yelled to throw it hard, I did, and it went directly up Feltus Street for a two-base error. We didn't win the championship, but we did learn to play with the big boys, which helped us later in our professional careers.

Jack's love of baseball goes back many years as he always listened to the ballgames on the radio. Allie Clark was Jack's hero, and Allie took Jack to Bears Stadium in Newark to catch batting practice and meet the Triple-A players of the International League.

When Jack was a junior and senior in high school, he worked for the post office, delivering mail during the Christmas season, and still played basketball along with all the other students who delivered mail, thanks to Postmaster Downs. He also shoveled snow in front of the church.

Later, Jack played for the South Amboy AA, a South River team, and another club. During the summer of the 1948 season, Jack formed the South Amboy All-Star baseball team, who won the Middlesex County Freeholders Baseball Tournament. As winners, we were eligible to play and represent the County of Middlesex in the New Jersey Star Ledger Newspapers' Baseball Championship. Jack guided the team to winning the title at Newark Bears Stadium. This victory allowed the team to represent New Jersey in the AAABA Baseball Tournament in Johnstown, Pennsylvania. All the players who went to Johnstown were St. Mary's or Hoffman High School baseball players. Jack attended Holy Cross University and later transferred to Seton Hall University. He drove a taxi, and a wrecker for my father, and got up many early mornings to go out and tow in wrecked cars off highways #35 and #9, as well as in the City of South Amboy.

Jack McKeon is a leader of people. He coached the United States Air Force team from Sampson, New York to the Air Force championship in 1952. Oddly enough, I coached the Army baseball team in Germany to the European baseball championship in 1955.

Jack signed a professional baseball contract with a local Pittsburgh scout, Gene Thomas, and started his professional baseball career in 1949, playing for the Greenville, Alabama Pirates. The rest is baseball history! He won championships in many minor league cities, and has managed major league teams in Kansas City, Oakland, San Diego, Cincinnati and now the 2003 World Series Champions, the Florida Marlins.

Marge Gorczyca Talks About
Big Brother, Jack McKeon

Marge McKeon Gorczyca , Jack's younger sister is his biggest fan. Last October, she traveled all over the country during the NL Playoffs and the World Series to see her brother's lifetime dream become a reality.

"I remember him always listening to baseball games on the radio. As we were growing up, there was no TV. I traveled a lot with my parents to see him play in the minor leagues, mostly the Carolina Leagues. We'd go two or three times during the summer. It took a long while to get there. There were no super highways, just farmlands.

Growing up, he worked for my dad towing in wrecks and drove taxis, as well as working for the Post Office. My father owned a taxi business, garage, and parking lot. He and Patsy Vona leased the parking lot from the railroad, and Jack used to work there too. We all pitched in. We all drove the cab and took our turns helping my dad out.

It was a great accomplishment when Jack got called to the majors to manage. I just regret that my father wasn't alive to see him make it to the big leagues, but my mom saw him. My mother got to see him, but my father was the one who really pushed him to be where he is today, and didn't live to see him make it."

She recalled very vividly "Jack McKeon Day" at Yankee Stadium in 1973:

"It was a big day. Tom Ryan put the event together. Our family was there. My mom, my sister when she was alive, and we all came back to my house that night, and I had a big party out in the back for those who worked on the "Jack McKeon Day." Then Jack had to go home that night, because as manager, he was in charge of the team, and had to be sure that everybody was in for curfew."

In 2003, Marge had a busy year, as her big brother came back to manage the Florida Marlins. "I always thought Jack would come out of retirement. He just couldn't be sitting there idle. He was helping out with his grandkids, but that's still not the same. He's the "Energizer Bunny." I went to all the World Series games. My friends were all Yankee fans, and when they saw he was in the World Series, they all went for the Marlins. Everybody you talk to thinks he's a great guy, and they're just so happy after all these years he really made it.

I don't think he's going to give up managing. I think he's going to keep on going and going. He has a great relationship with the young ballplayers today, and believes in not screaming at them. You go out there and play the best you can, have fun! It seems like it's working."

McKeon's sister feels that his greatest moment in his 50-plus years career in professional baseball was when, "He got the call to manage the Marlins. You figure, once you're retired, who wants an older person to manage, but when he got that call in May, I think that was the greatest moment."

As always, Marge has continued to follow her brother and the Florida Marlins closely. "I just can't wait to get home and put that game on and see Jack. I don't wanna miss it. I even got the Sports package so that I can see every game possible. It's great! I'm just so proud of Jack!"

2003-McKeon (c) with two of his biggest fans, sister Marge Gorczyca (l) and her husband Ron Gorczyca (r).

Bill Beck (r), McKeon's long-time friend and co-worker, was instrumental in getting Jack (l) the job as Marlins' manager in 2003. Beck is Florida's Director, Team Travel

High School Teammates And Opponents Remember Jack

Ed O'Brien

Ed and Johnny O'Brien were probably the most famous twins in America in the early 1950's. Their story is so interesting that it should have been made into a great sports movie. Hopefully it will be someday.

The O'Brien's played with Jack on his first organized team, the McKeon's Boys Club in the early 1940's, and all through St. Mary's (South Amboy, N.J.) High School baseball and basketball teams. In 1948, John and Eddie starred with McKeon on the state championship basketball squad.

The O'Brien Twins went on to become national stars in baseball and basketball at Seattle University, where they were All-Americans, and established all types of records in both sports.

After graduation, they were signed by the Pittsburgh Pirates as "Bonus Babies," and on May 10, 1953, made major league history, when they started at shortstop and second base in a game at the Polo Grounds against the New York Giants. It marked the first time that identical twins played together in baseball. They remained teammates until 1958, when Johnny was traded to the St. Louis Cardinals. They held the major league record for double plays by brothers until the Ripkens, Cal and Billy broke it several years ago.

After their big league careers, the twins found much success in business, politics, and all phases of life. Their hard work ethic, determination and dedication truly shows how one can succeed in America.

Ed remembered the good old days with Jack:

"Jack, my brother John and I may have been the first to play in an indoor "stadium." When it rained, Jack's dad would clear his trucks out of his garage and we would hit in there. He never charged us for the broken windows.

Over the years, I got to see Jack in San Diego and Chicago. We, (My wife Terry and I) had lunch with him while he was managing the Padres. That morning, his booster club presented him with a Grandfather's Clock. I commented that he was so popular, he should run for Mayor. His comment: 'I'd probably win.'

Jack was the block setter on the high school basketball team. He didn't shoot much, feeling rebounding and setting blocks were his strengths. He was good at it. I might comment that we all started playing basketball late. We didn't even make the team in our frosh year.

Baseball was our game and Jack loved it! That's why his success doesn't surprise me. After high school, he went to Holy Cross and we ended up in Seattle. Our paths didn't cross during our playing days. The closest was when he managed in Vancouver B.C., 2 1/2 hours north of Seattle.

I could not be happier for Jack. He has earned his place among baseball's best

226

managers. No one has put more time and energy into the national pastime."

Leo Kedzierski

In the 1940's, he played baseball on The McKeon's Boys Club Youth League team, varsity baseball at St. Mary's, and also on the NJ Amateur State Championship club with Jack McKeon. Leo went on to play professional baseball for a few years in the minors.

He was kind enough to share some of his memories about Jack:

"We go back to the McKeon Boys Club. His father helped put it together. As we got older and played in high school, he was a tremendous catcher, with a very quick release, and they couldn't steal off of him because he got rid of the ball so quick. He was very intelligent and knew how to handle pitchers. He was right on top of what was going on. He occasionally got a base hit that would help.

Jack and Leo both signed professional contracts in the same month in 1949, McKeon with the Pittsburgh Pirates, and Kedzierski with the New York Giants.

Leo recalled that, "In October or November that year when it was getting cold, we would go to the field, which had dim lights, and hit ground balls. We also did wind sprints. It kept us in good condition for camp the next year. Jack was a very hard worker.

I remember when he was managing Oakland, and my wife and I, and another couple went to Yankee Stadium to see him. I asked him how he was making out with the club, and he said, 'How'd you like to manage this bunch?'

Jack is sincere and can handle people very well, and I am glad the Marlins are doing well."

Jerry Connors

Jerry Connors played baseball and basketball with Jack McKeon at St. Mary's High School, and along with McKeon, was also a member of the 1948 New Jersey Amateur Baseball Championship club. Jerry is a retired Lieutenant Colonel, who served for over 20 years in the United States Marine Corps. He had many fond memories of his teammate:

"I can remember in grammar school when I was in the 7th grade and Jack was in the 8th. The nuns scheduled a game for us during school hours. I was playing left field, and Jack hit one by the brick wall near the tennis courts, and I caught it. He thought he'd hit a home run.

As a freshman, I was on the team, and Jack, a sophomore was the number 1 catcher. Mario Birardi was the backup catcher. I didn't play during my sophomore year, but that summer, Jack was managing Jerome's Tavern team in the City League with "Trip" Cheeseman. It was a men's league with kids playing old guys Jack could have played with any team. He was in demand, and along with "Mikey" Carroll, was one of the best catchers around. Well, Jack needed pitchers and he tried me out at the old St. Mary's schoolyard. He said, 'You look good enough. We'll get you a suit.' I got a Cardinal shirt with two cardinals on it. We had the two O'Briens, and Jim Cassidy who was about 30 years old. I pitched a couple of games. Abby's Tavern was the best team in the league. Some of the best players in the league were the Zebros, "Lefty" Mackiel, Jankowski, Ray Stockton, Jim Croddick, Reggie Carney and "Red" Connors. Jack was the manager (Only 15 years old at the time), and we won a few games, beating Nelson's Tavern and Mechanicsville.

In '48, Jack's senior year, the basketball team did very well and won the Catholic School State Championship. Jack was a leader and skillful ball handler. He was the '48 version of a point guard. He could also rebound very well. He held the team together. We hung out quite a bit at local stores like Frank O'Connor's.

Jack did very well on the 1948 South Amboy All Stars, the team that won the New Jersey State Amateur Baseball title. He was regarded as a very good catcher. It didn't surprise me when he signed with the Pittsburgh Pirates. Gene Thomas was the local scout that signed him. I remember when he came home after his first spring training. He looked like a million bucks.

Around 1951 before Spring Training, Jack decided with Leo Kedzierski and myself that we'd go on a 20-mile walk from South Amboy to Matawan and back. By 1953, we were both out of South Amboy and went our separate ways.

I ran into him briefly in Elon, North Carolina. I was on the baseball and basketball teams at Belmont Abbey with Frank "Butch" O'Brien, and Jack was living down there and found out we were there. He came over and talked to us. The next time I saw him was at Yankee Stadium for "Jack McKeon Day," but didn't get a chance to talk to him.

I then saw him about 20 years ago at Philadelphia when he was GM of the San Diego Padres. I called him at the hotel and told him I was going to the game and was going to stop and see him. I went down in the fourth inning to where he was sitting, and he introduced me to his wife. He later came up and sat with us for an inning and talked for about 10 or 15 minutes. That was very nice.

I'm not surprised with his great success. He always had the ability to work with people, to run a team. He was my first catcher. No disrespect for the others, but he was the best I ever had. He could handle pitchers. He was that good! He never really got on you. If you walked two or three guys, he'd try to settle you down.

I was surprised when he came back to manage Florida in 2003. I was also very happy he was doing it, and did so well.

Ray Wisniewski

Ray Wisniewski was a talented baseball player with Hoffman High School, arch-rival of Jack McKeon's St. Mary's team. After high school, he was asked to sign with the Philadelphia Phillies farm system. Even as a teenager, McKeon knew how to judge players and recruited Wisniewski to play for his South Amboy All Stars team that went on to win the 1948 New Jersey Amateur championship. Ray recalled the good old days:

"Jack was always a winner. He was always the manager of the team. He knew how to win. He was a good catcher and could hit. The McKeon Boys Club was the only team in town with uniforms.

I remember the All Star team playing in *The Star Ledger* Tournament and going to Pennsylvania. We won our first three, but ran out of pitching.

When asked about Jack's huge success, Ray said, "He did great! The odds aren't that good, but he was always a pusher. He was known as "Trader Jack" at San Diego."

John "Skeets" Skarzynski

John "Skeets" Skarzynski, was a standout baseball and basketball player for Hoffman High School, local rival to McKeon's St. Mary's High School team. "Skeets" played with Jack on the South Amboy All-Stars, the team that copped the 1948 New Jersey Amateur State Championship, and also against McKeon in the South Amboy City Series games.

"He always beat me. I played against him in high school, and in the minors when I was with Danville and he was with Greenville, and he always beat me. We were two Yankees playing in Rebel country back in those days.

The thing I admired about Jack is that I was always his backup catcher and said 'Someday I'm gonna catch up with you and take your place.' When he got older and moved up, I took his place. It was a hard job to fill that position. Jack was a helluva catcher and a good line drive, contact hitter. He was the leader. He put the South Amboy All-Stars together. He practically managed the team. He was a natural then. He gave Richie Ryan (Manager) a lot of input. It just shows you the guy was a natural. He never gave up on the game. He's a natural for talent. When you're out of the game for a couple of years, you lose touch with the talent in the game. Jack picked up where he left off."

John Wojcik

John pitched for neighboring Sayreville High School against Jack, and also crossed paths with him in the minors in the Alabama State League. He said:

"I played against Jack McKeon in high school and also in the Alabama State League in 1949. He was in the Pittsburgh Pirates chain. He was a good, smart catcher, who called all the plays.

*Jack catching up on hometown news in The South Amboy-Sayreville Times, before
the Marlins took on the Philadelphia Phillies at their new Citizens Bank Park on
April 21, 2004.*

Florida Marlins' hitting coach Bill Robinson (l) and Jack (r) during BP in 2004

McKeon contemplates an answer to a New York sportswriter's question at Shea Stadium in 2004.

The Marlins' skipper in the dugout at Shea Stadium during the New York-Florida game on June 5, 2004.

*Jack (l) pays a mound visit to pitcher Tommy Phelps (c) and catcher
Matt Treanor (r) during the Marlins-Mets contest at Shea Stadium on June 5, 2004.*

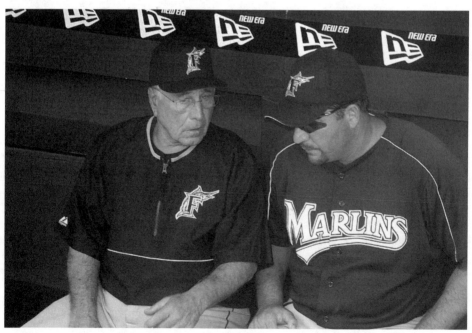

*Pitching coach Wayne Rosenthal (r) and McKeon go over pitching strategies prior to a
game in 2004.*

Florida Marlins' owner Jeffrey Loria (l) and Jack McKeon (r) prior to a Mets- Marlins game at New York in 2004.

Jack McKeon (r) and his boyhood idol, former Yankee, Allie Clark (l) enjoyed the festivities at the New Jersey Sportswriters Association's Annual Banquet in January 2004.

Jack waves to fans at Shea Stadium.

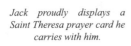

Jack proudly displays a Saint Theresa prayer card he carries with him.

Veterans Park, Home of Jack McKeon Field was named to honor the Vets and Jack by his hometown in October 2000. The field was previously called Veterans Field by some residents, and Tigers Field by others. Jack spent countless hours as a youth here, playing the game he loves so much.

Benefit Dinner Honoring

Jack McKeon

Salute to the Flag .... Eddie McKeon
Opening Prayer .... Fr. Simon and Invited Guests
Introduction of the Family .... Marge Gorczyca

Awards

South Amboy Irishman of the Year .... Ancient Order of Hibernians
Recognition Award .... South Amboy Police Department
Special Recognition .... Cardinal McCarrick High School
Special Recognition .... St. Mary Elementary School
Special Recognition .... St. Mary Athletic Association
Emerald Society Award .... Pete Kenny

Municipal Awards

Introduction .... Mayor John T. O'Leary
Proclamation:
New Jersey State Senate and Assembly .... Senator Joseph Vitale
                                                       and Assemblyman John Wisniewski
Proclamation:
Middlesex County Freeholders .... Stephen Pete Dalina
Proclamation:
City of South Amboy .... Mayor John T. O'Leary

Our Honored Guest

Introduction .... Allie Clark
Honored Guest .... Jack McKeon
Closing Comments .... Patricia Cahill, Principal
                                                   St. Mary Elementary School

This is the official program for the Tribute/Dinner Benefit held in Jack's honor in South Amboy on January 23, 2004.

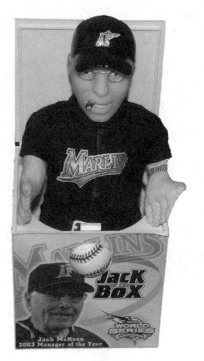

This bobble head collectible shows Jack in a Greensboro uniform. This was given away as a promotion at a Greensboro Bats game and sponsored by Murphy/Wainer Orthopedic Specialists. Jack played briefly for the Greensboro Patriots in '55.

Jack In The Box was one of the Marlins' most popular promotional days of 2004 at Pro Player Stadium. The highly collectible Jack In The Box featured Florida manager Jack McKeon. The event was sponsored by Tenet South Florida.

This is the official poster that advertised "Jack McKeon Day" at Yankee Stadium in 1973.
(Poster courtesy of Tom Ryan)

This is the special collectors page, given away by The South Amboy-Sayreville Times newspaper at the Tribute/Dinner Fundrasier held in Jack's honor on January 23, 2004. (Collectors page designed by Brian Stratton, Scans & More)

237

Jack with his son-in-law, Greg Booker, who was a big league pitcher and pitching coach with the San Diego Padres.

Pictured at a St. Mary's High School Class of '48 reunion are members Alfie O'Connor, John and Ed O'Brien, Angie Sobczak and Jack (r).

Jack McKeon wears the white fire chief's hat as he visits with members of the Protection Engine Company No. 1 in South Amboy, New Jersey.

The multi-talented McKeon tries his hand at barbecuing ribs at Protection Engine Company No. 1 along with Satski's Famous Spare Rib Kings Chefs. The firefighters hold the barbecue as a company fundraiser.

Jack and his wife Carol stand next to the beautiful Mercedes convertible, which was given to him as a gift from Marlins' owner, Jeffrey Loria for guiding the club to the World Series.

One of the world's biggest collectors, Al Gomolka Jr. (l), adds to his sports memorabilia, as Jack signs an item for him. (Photo by Brian Stratton)

1949-Jack's in the on-deck circle during his rookie year in pro ball at Greenville, Alabama.

In 2004, Jack McKeon won both his 2,000th professional game, and 900th in the major leagues.
(Photo courtesy of Florida Marlins)

Jack McKeon's Minor League Batting Record

Year	Club	G	AB	R	H	2B	3B	HR	RBI	Avg.
1949	Greenville	116	390	54	98	12	1	1	49	.251
1950	York	1	3	0	1	0	0	0	0	.333
1950	Gloversville	72	209	18	45	5	0	0	14	.215
1951	*In Military Service*									
1952	Hutchinson	116	338	42	78	10	1	4	40	.218
1953	Burlington	140	474	46	86	19	2	6	52	.181
1954	Burlington	17	30	1	4	0	0	0	2	.133
1954	Hutchinson	46	140	18	29	5	0	1	13	.207
1955	Fay. Greens	59	172	20	29	3	0	1	17	.169
1956	Missoula	113	370	44	63	8	0	0	29	.170
1957	Missoula	102	299	37	65	7	0	4	40	.217
1958	Missoula	108	354	49	93	15	0	8	51	.263
1959	Fox Cities	11	20	1	2	0	0	0	1	.100
	Minor League Totals	*901*	*2799*	*330*	*593*	*84*	*4*	*25*	*308*	*.212*

Jack McKeon's Minor League Managerial Record

Year	Team	League	Won	Lost	Pct.	Finish
1955	Fayetteville	Carolina	70	67	.511	3rd
1956	Missoula	Pioneer	61	71	.462	7th
1957	Missoula	Pioneer (1st Half)	26	35	.426	6th
		(2nd Half)	36	29	.554	3rd
1958	Missoula	Pioneer (1st Half)	34	29	.540	4th
		(2nd Half)	36	30	.545	3rd
1959	Fox Cities	Three-I (1st Half)	26	39	.400	7th
		(2nd Half)	33	28	.541	4th
1960	Wilson	Carolina (1st Half)	36	34	.514	3rd
		(2nd Half)	37	31	.544	2nd
1961	Wilson	Carolina (1st Half)	41	28	.594	1st
		(2nd Half)	42	28	.600	1st
1962	Vancouver	Pacific Coast	72	79	.477	7th
1963	Dallas-Ft Worth	Pacific Coast	79	79	.500	3rd
1964	Atlanta	International	19	42	.311	--
1968	High Point	Carolina	69	71	.493	*2nd
1969	Omaha	American Association	85	55	.607	1st
1970	Omaha	American Association	73	65	.529	1st
1971	Omaha	American Association	69	70	.496	3rd
1972	Omaha	American Association	71	69	.507	2nd
1976	Richmond	International	69	71	.493	4th
1979	Denver	American Assoication	62	73	.459	3rd
	Minor League Totals		*1146*	*1123*	*.505*	

243

Jack McKeon's Major League Managerial Record
(As of October 15, 2004)

Year	Team	Games	Won	Lost	Pct.	Finish
1973	Kansas City	162	88	74	.543	2nd
1974	Kansas City	162	77	85	.475	5th
1975	Kansas City	96	50	46	.521	2nd
1977	Oakland	53	26	27	.491	7th
1978	Oakland	123	45	78	.366	6th
1988	San Diego	115	67	48	.583	3rd
1989	San Diego	162	89	73	.549	2nd
1990	San Diego	80	37	43	.462	5th
1997	Cincinnati	63	33	30	.524	3rd
1998	Cincinnati	162	77	85	.475	4th
1999	Cincinnati	163	96	67	.589	2nd
2000	Cincinnati	162	85	77	.525	2nd
2003	Florida	124	75	49	.605	2nd*
2004	Florida	162	83	79	.512	3rd

*Won World Series Championship over the New York Yankees, 4-2.

Jack McKeon's Major League Managerial Record
Lifetime Totals By Team

Team	Games	Won	Lost	Pct.
Kansas City	420	215	205	.512
Oakland	176	71	105	.403
San Diego	357	193	164	.541
Cincinnati	550	291	259	.529
Florida	286	158	128	.552
Totals	*1789*	*928*	*861*	*.519*

Acknowledgements

I would like to thank everyone, who in any way, shape or form helped me in my research for this book, or with interviews or information, and especially, Brian Stratton, owner of Scans & More for his brilliant cover design and outstanding job with the pictures. Also, for his overall dedication and always being just a phone call away. Brian's wife, Phyllis Stratton has also done a superb job with the layout and her editorial expertise. Thank you!

Jack's sister, Marge Gorczyca and his brother Bill "Biff" McKeon, were tremendous in their help in supplying old photos and information. Ed O'Brien was kind enough to loan us his outstanding scrapbook with great team photos from the 1940's, which we used in the book. I would be remiss if I did not extend a special thank you to my dear friends with the Florida Marlins Major League Baseball Club, especially Owner Jeffrey Loria, and Steve Copses, Director of Media Relations, for being so helpful over the last two years, when we were covering Jack and the Marlins, and also for the photos. You have always made us feel welcome at your home in Florida, and I can honestly say that I feel like I am part of the Marlins' baseball family. Thank you, again for your kindness and hospitality!

Jay Horwitz, Vice President of Media Relations for the New York Mets, has always been more than helpful and kind to us at Shea Stadium. Thank you, Jay and your fine staff for your cooperation, understanding and support through the years.

Another heartfelt thank you is extended to Leigh Tobin and Mary Ann Gettis of the Philadelphia Phillies for providing us with access to cover Marlins' games. Thank you to the Cincinnati Reds and also Kansas City Royals for the photos of Jack McKeon.

My sister, Madeline "Maddie" Bowerman has always been encouraging and supportive in all of my endeavors, and I thank her for believing in me.

Last, but far from least, a special thank you to all of my good friends (You know who you are) for always listening, and giving me moral support. I certainly have been blessed to have so many wonderful people in my life.

Photo Credits